DEAD ENDS!

Flukes, Flops & Failures
That Sparked Medical Marvels

ALSO BY LINDSEY FITZHARRIS AND ADRIAN TEAL

Plague-Busters! Medicine's Battles with History's Deadliest Diseases

DEAD ENDS!

Flukes, Flops & Failures That Sparked Medical Marvels

LINDSEY FITZHARRIS and **ADRIAN TEAL**

Illustrated by ADRIAN TEAL

BLOOMSBURY
CHILDREN'S BOOKS

NEW YORK · LONDON · OXFORD · NEW DELHI · SYDNEY

BLOOMSBURY CHILDREN'S BOOKS
Bloomsbury Publishing Inc., part of Bloomsbury Publishing Plc
1359 Broadway, New York, NY 10018
50 Bedford Square, London, WC1B 3DP, UK
Bloomsbury Publishing Ireland Limited, 29 Earlsfort Terrace, Dublin 2, D02 AY28, Ireland

BLOOMSBURY, BLOOMSBURY CHILDREN'S BOOKS, and the Diana logo
are trademarks of Bloomsbury Publishing Plc

First published in the United States of America in October 2025
by Bloomsbury Children's Books

Text copyright © 2025 by Lindsey Fitzharris and Adrian Teal
Illustrations copyright © 2025 by Adrian Teal

Bloomsbury books may be purchased for business or promotional use. For information on bulk purchases
please contact Macmillan Corporate and Premium Sales Department at specialmarkets@macmillan.com

This book is for informational purposes only and does not make any medical recommendations.
The treatments, remedies, and experiments described in this book should not be tried at home.

Library of Congress Cataloging-in-Publication Data
available upon request
ISBN 978-1-5476-1502-5 (hardcover) • ISBN 978-1-5476-1503-2 (e-book)

Book design by John Candell
Printed and bound in China
2 4 6 8 10 9 7 5 3 1

To find out more about our authors and books visit www.bloomsbury.com and sign up for our newsletters.
For product safety–related questions contact productsafety@bloomsbury.com.

To our mentors, Dr. Margaret Pelling and Roger Law

• TABLE OF CONTENTS •

DEAD ENDS!

Flukes, Flops & Failures
That Sparked Medical Marvels

*Albert Einstein (attributed)

INTRODUCTION

THE VICTORIAN SURGEON ROBERT Liston was a giant of his day—both professionally and literally. At six feet two inches, he was eight inches taller than most British men. He was famous for his brute strength and his speed at a time when both were crucial to his patients' survival.

Robert was known as the "Fastest Knife" in London. Medical students and members of the public would cram themselves into the operating theater to watch him remove arms and legs. He could lop off a limb in less than thirty seconds, and a spectator might miss a gory detail if they looked away for even a moment. In order to keep both hands free, he would clasp the bloody knife between his teeth while he slashed and

sawed. Today, we would consider this disgustingly unhygienic, but Robert didn't because he and his fellow surgeons didn't know about germs.

Robert was a pioneer in the operating theater. For example, he invented a method for cutting through a limb that left behind a U-shaped flap of tissue that could be used to cover the end of the bone. This totally changed the way amputations were performed. He also created what later became known as the "Liston knife," which had a long, straight blade that was sharpened on both edges. This made cutting through skin, muscle, and tissue much faster. And he invented a type of leg splint for setting broken bones that would be recommended in first aid manuals for more than one hundred years!

But Robert experienced his fair share of failure as well. His speed was both a gift and a curse. His most famous mishap involved an operation during which he worked so fast that he took off three of his assistant's fingers and, while switching blades, slashed a spectator's coat. The unlucky bystander died from fright on the spot, and both the assistant and the patient later kicked the bucket due to infection. It's the only surgery in history said to have had a 300 percent fatality rate!

Despite Robert's failures, he was still considered one of the most successful surgeons of his day. He was fearless, and he often agreed to operate on patients for whom surgery was a last resort. In doing so, he saved many lives.

Robert Liston is a shining example of what we're going to show you in this book, which is that success and failure are often two sides of the same coin. Most of the time, you can't have one without the other. You'll also see how something that's hailed as a medical success at one time in history can be thrown out with the trash in another, as ideas, understanding, and experience all develop over the ages. This is a normal part of what we call the "scientific method." It's okay to change our minds as new evidence and information become available. In fact, being open to new ideas is essential to scientific progress!

Of course, some disasters never had an upside. The history of medicine is littered with unethical, unhygienic, unscientific, and just-plain-wrong practices. But you'll see how sometimes a major foul-up led unexpectedly to an incredible breakthrough. Doctors came to a better understanding of the human body, and the best ways to treat it, through centuries of failures, mistakes, and misunderstandings. Plus, we'll show that nobody is immune to messing up. Even medical geniuses balanced their triumphs with a healthy number of false starts and downright wrong-headedness.

We have put on our rubber gloves, grabbed a knife, and rummaged around in the guts of history, pulling out the juiciest examples of stuff that went very, *very* badly wrong. Each of our chapters explains how medicine has treated different parts of the body through the ages—with differing degrees of success.

So, lean in close and watch carefully. Just be wary of that flashing blade!

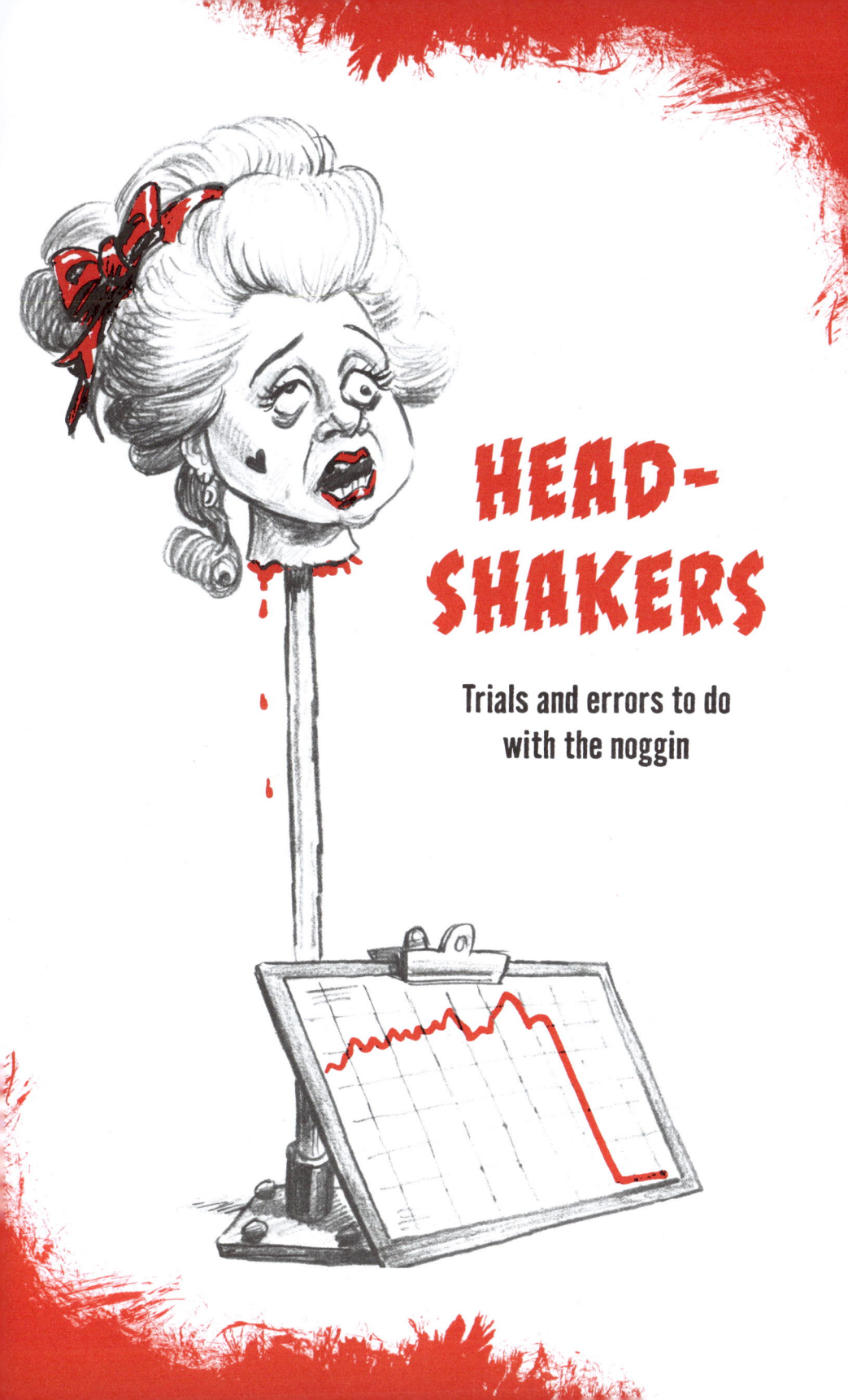

HEAD-SHAKERS

Trials and errors to do with the noggin

IT OFTEN TOOK MEDICAL SCIENCE a long time to turn a wrongheaded approach into a world-changing success story. Take, for example, the question of exactly when someone should be declared dead.

People feared being pronounced dead when they were only unconscious—nobody wanted to be buried alive! Some doctors used the lack of a pulse to determine death. Others felt that death could only be confirmed once the body began to rot. In the eighteenth century, the head was shoved right into the middle of the debate about how to tell the difference between "absolute" and "apparent" death, leading to some truly weird experiments.

In October of 1791, the French government ordered that all those sentenced to death should be beheaded. And this was all thanks to the advice of a doctor! His name was Joseph-Ignace Guillotin, and he had the strange idea that a mechanical chopping

JOSEPH-IGNACE GUILLOTIN

device for executing criminals humanely and quickly would be a useful first step toward ending the death penalty. Although beheading may not sound humane, it would replace hanging, which could be a horribly long death as the condemned slowly choked at the end of a rope.

The guillotine was born, but it led to terrible bloodshed during the French Revolution, in which thousands of people lost their heads. Dr. Guillotin failed miserably in his goal to abolish the death penalty. After the good doctor's death in 1814, his family asked the government to rename the device as they didn't want to be associated with it. Unfortunately for the Guillotin family, their request was turned down, so the family changed its name instead.

As soon as the guillotine was put into use, arguments broke out over whether its victims were really dead at the moment their heads came off.

After a woman named Charlotte Corday was beheaded in 1793, the executioner slapped her, and witnesses swore they saw her blush! Her staring eyes also suggested she was aware of her terrible situation. Someone even wrote to Dr. Guillotin to ask if he

In England, severed heads were often put on spikes and displayed on London Bridge. Many people believed these gross trophies had healing powers, and some even thought drinking from a human skull could cure ailments. In the sixteenth century, a number of Germans working at the Royal Mint in London fell suddenly ill (likely due to breathing in the copper fumes from coin making). To try to heal them, the heads on London Bridge were taken down, the flesh was boiled off, and the skulls were made into cups for the sick workers. Some of the men recovered, but many of them died. Surprise, surprise!

was certain that a person's feelings and personality died as soon as they were decapitated. Others soon set out to find an answer.

The first to reportedly investigate whether the guillotine caused immediate death was a Dr. Séguret, who experimented on guillotined heads during the French Revolution. In several cases, he exposed victims' eyes to the sun and noted that they quickly closed by themselves in a startling way. He pricked one of the severed head's tongues with a sharp tool called a lancet, noting that the tongue immediately shot back into the mouth, and that the face winced as if in pain. Dr. Séguret, along with others who performed similar experiments, believed that the severed heads did show signs of life shortly after being chopped off. But it was pretty clear then, and even more so today, that death will quickly follow when your head is separated from your shoulders!

Nearly a hundred years later, in 1884, the French government began handing over the severed heads of criminals to a doctor named Jean-Baptiste Vincent Laborde, who believed he could "cure" death. Apparently, he had been able to revive victims of drowning, poisoning, and strangulation, along with a dog and a guinea pig. After those reported successes, he began a series of experiments on severed human heads, drilling holes into their skulls and pushing needles into their brains. He then ran an electrical current through the needles in an attempt to trigger a response from the nervous system. In one case, a head reportedly opened an eye, as if trying to figure out where it was and why it was being put through such horrors!

There are many questions that everyone involved in these stories totally failed to answer. Firstly, if the heads of criminals truly did live on for a while, wasn't all the poking and prodding and electrocuting just prolonging their suffering? And what, if anything, were you supposed to do to help a "still-living" head in the long term, after it had been parted from its body?! Should you even try to revive the heads, especially given that they were from people condemned to death? And what did any of this tell us that could be useful medically?

Well, as grim as all this was, these early experiments did lead to deeper investigations into resuscitation science, which led to the development of vital life-saving technology on which the world relies today. And a dead end (or a head!) may still offer important lessons that can point medicine in the right direction.

It wasn't only dead heads that contributed to medical progress. Those whose heads were still attached to their bodies offered plenty of opportunities to study the noggin, too. Believe it or not, people have been undergoing really delicate surgery on their heads for a very long time. Take, for example, this story involving a prince, a slippery staircase, and a dead saint . . .

In 1562, Don Carlos—who was the only son of King Philip II of Spain—fell down a flight of stairs while chasing a servant. At the bottom of the steps, he slammed against a door and split the back of his head open. His doctors bandaged the injury, but the wound became infected and Carlos grew gravely ill. Eleven days after the accident, six doctors met to discuss the case. Among them was a very famous fellow named Andreas Vesalius, who later became known as the founder of modern anatomy. He and his five colleagues decided to widen the wound to release the pus that had gathered under the scalp. But the prince's condition worsened further. The docs then rubbed powders, plasters, ointments, and herbal preparations on the injury. Someone even laid the body of a Catholic saint by Carlos's bed in the hopes it might have healing powers.

When all of this failed, Andreas and another doctor decided

ANDREAS VESALIUS

to drill a separate hole in the prince's skull to relieve the pressure caused by swelling. Over the course of several weeks, Carlos's health improved, and three months after the accident, he was declared cured.

Don Carlos wasn't the first person in history to have a hole drilled into his head—not by a LONG stretch. Trepanation is the name for the medical procedure in which a small piece of a patient's skull is cut out, exposing the brain underneath, and it had been around for thousands of years before the prince cracked his coconut at the bottom of a staircase.

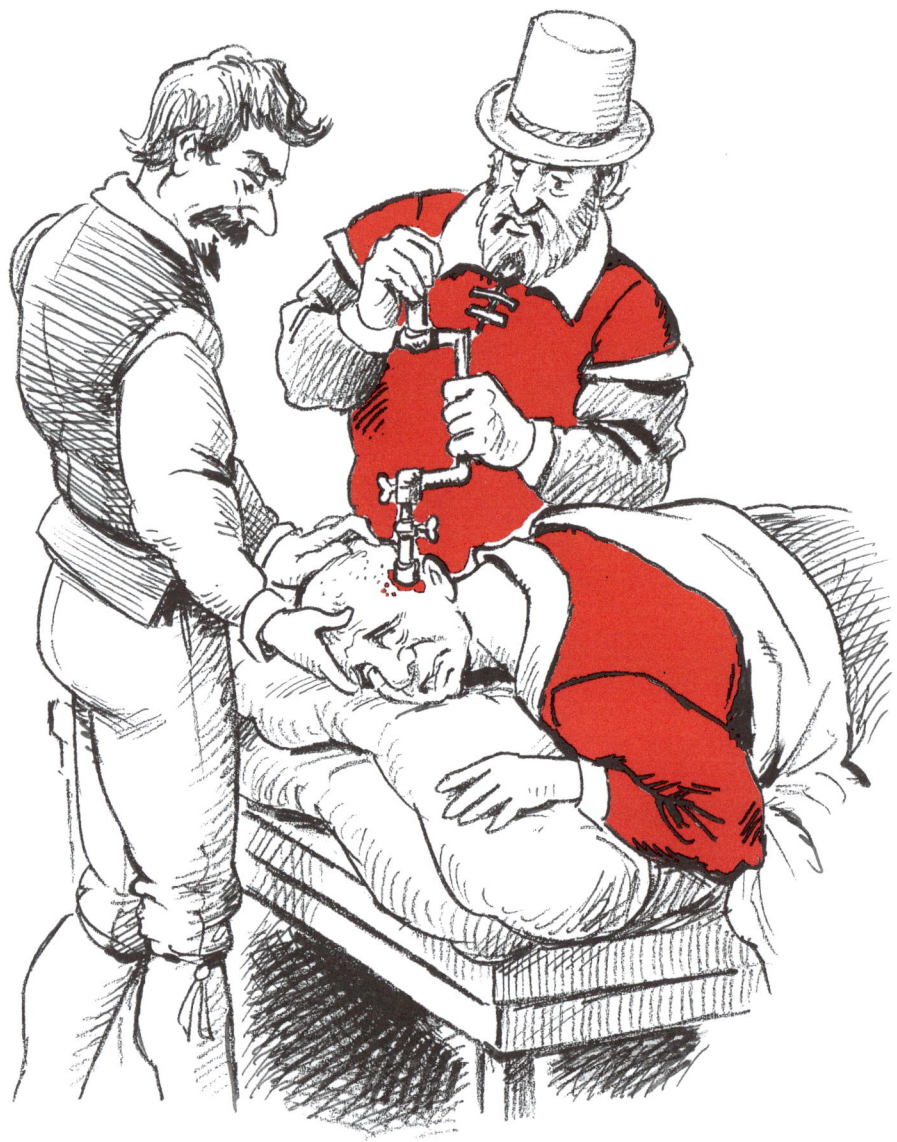

The word "trepanation" comes from the ancient Greek word for a drill or borer, but the practice seems to date back at least eight thousand years! And it happened all over the world. We know of historical cases in Peru, Hungary, Egypt, and China, to name a few. In fact, Hua Tuo, the first known Chinese surgeon, who died around 208 CE, is thought to have trepanned many heads in his time.

So, why were our ancestors letting people punch holes in their skulls? After all, this was before anesthesia, and it would have been a really painful and dangerous operation. Well, in earlier centuries, trepanation may have been carried out to allow "demons" to escape from sick or troubled people, or simply to deal with headaches. In more recent centuries, the procedure was used to relieve pressure or drain blood caused by head injuries.

And the survival rate was surprisingly high. Archeologists have found many trepanned skulls, which is how we know this practice has been carried out for thousands of years. Many of the holes in these skulls show evidence of healing around the edges, meaning that the patients didn't die straight after the operation. In fact, a seventeenth-century Dutch prince, Philip of Nassau, managed to survive being trepanned twenty-seven times!

In the seventeenth century, a Russian surgeon repaired a defect in a soldier's skull by implanting a fragment of dog bone into it. The Church condemned the practice and banned the soldier from all their religious services as a result. When the man asked for the procedure to be reversed, his surgeon discovered that the soldier's own bone had grown around the graft and it couldn't be removed.

Trepanation still happens today. It's now known as "burr hole surgery," and it's used to treat subdural hematomas, which is a tongue-twisting term for a bleed in the gap between the brain and the skull. One or more small holes are drilled into the bone, and a rubber tube is used to drain the blood. No demons are harmed in the process of this operation.

Curing headaches didn't always involve using trepanation to turn your skull into a sieve, though. Nearly two thousand years ago, Scribonius Largus, doctor to the Roman emperor Claudius, took an unusual interest in the torpedo fish. This is a terrifying animal that can send up to 220 volts of electricity through anyone who touches it—enough to stun, disable, or even kill a human being.

Scribonius had heard of a man who claimed he'd been cured of gout (a painful disease of the joints) after he accidentally stepped on a torpedo fish while strolling on a beach. Curious about these claims, Scribonius began performing experiments with the fish. It wasn't long

In the eighteenth century, the Scottish surgeon John Hunter studied the anatomy of the torpedo fish. He discovered that the organs responsible for pumping out the electric current were several hundred stacks of flat, jelly-filled disks. Three decades later, the fish inspired the Italian physicist Alexandro Volta to use the stack arrangement, first discovered by Hunter, to create the first electrochemical battery.

before he was recommending that the emperor place a torpedo fish on his forehead to cure him of his chronic headaches.

Word of Scribonius's head-zapping methods soon spread, and other doctors began recommending the electric currents of the torpedo fish to their patients. The practice persisted for hundreds of years, and was even used by European doctors to treat headaches as late as the eighteenth century. It's not a great idea to expose yourself to such a powerful shock, but today, we know that electrical current can be therapeutic. Doctors are still not totally clear why it can be helpful when treating certain disorders. But just because something is a medical mystery doesn't necessarily make it a dead end.

Medical failures often happen when doctors cling on tightly to bad ideas and harmful beliefs for a long time—sometimes for thousands of years. A good example of this involves another part of the skull: the teeth!

In the past, many people believed in the existence of the "tooth worm": a little creature that caused toothaches by boring holes in human teeth. This seems like nonsense to us today, of course, but if you think about it, there's a kind of logic to it. After all, people were troubled by worms in their bowels, lice on their bodies, and fleas in their scalps, so why should their mouths have been any different?

Tooth worms have a long history, first appearing in a text from Sumer (now part of modern-day Iraq) written around 5000 BCE. Other mentions of tooth worms can be found in China, Egypt, and India dating to long before the belief finally took root in Western Europe, in the early Middle Ages.

The treatment of tooth worms varied depending on how bad the patient's pain was. Often, doctors would try to "smoke" the worm out. They would heat a mixture of beeswax and the seeds of a plant called henbane on a piece of iron, and then direct the fumes into the tooth cavity with a funnel. Afterward, they would fill the hole with powdered henbane seed, and a plant gum known as mastic. This may have given some temporary relief because henbane has painkilling properties. But if the "worm" (and the pain) remained, the achy tooth had to be removed altogether. Dentists may sometimes still pull achy teeth today, but back then, some tooth-pullers mistook the pulpy nerves in teeth for the guilty worms, and extracted both the tooth and the nerve. This would have been an extremely painful procedure before anesthetics were discovered!

The whole idea of tooth worms finally came under attack in the eighteenth century, when the Frenchman Pierre Fauchard—known today as the father of modern dentistry—suggested that tooth decay was linked to eating sugar.

In the 1890s, the American dentist Willoughby D. Miller took this idea a step further, and found that little creatures actually were to blame! It was just on a smaller scale than people had thought. He showed through a series of experiments that bacteria living inside the mouth produce acids that dissolve the outer layer of teeth when in the presence of certain carbs, like sugar.

Despite these discoveries, many people continued to believe in the existence of tooth worms into the twentieth century. Experts may work hard to shoot down outdated ideas, but people tend to cling to their beliefs, which often keeps them stuck in dead ends longer than they need to be.

A TASTE OF THEIR OWN MEDICINE . . .

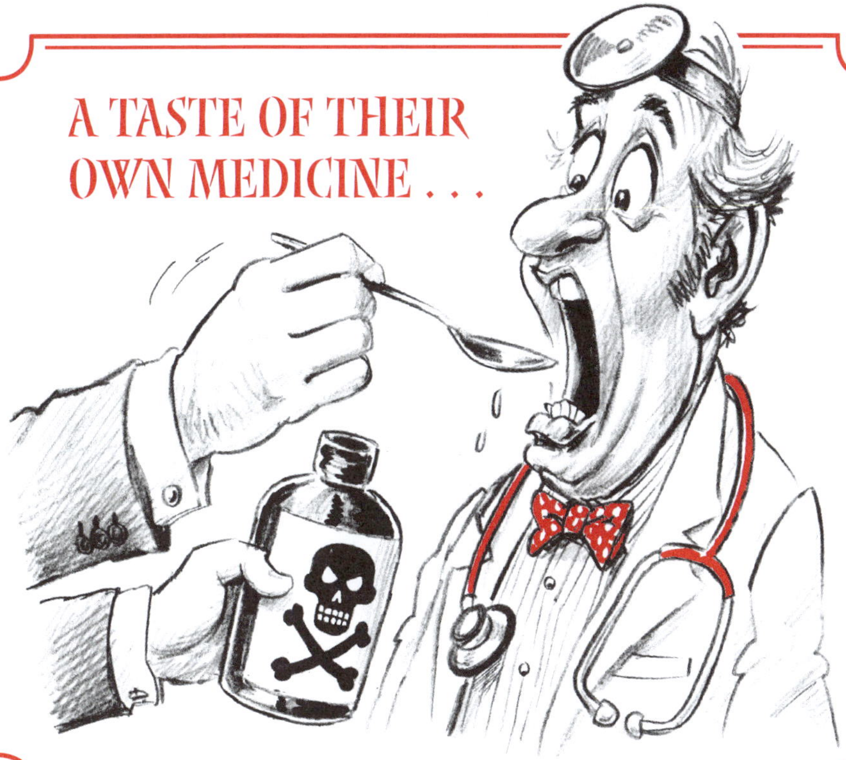

In 1828, William Burke and William Hare murdered sixteen people in the Scottish capital of Edinburgh. The two killers then sold the fresh corpses to surgeons who would otherwise have had a shortage of bodies to dissect in private anatomy schools dotted around the city.

Burke and Hare were eventually caught when one of their victims was discovered in the dissection room of Dr. Robert Knox, who had been buying many of the suspiciously fresh bodies from the two men over the past several months. After the pair were arrested, Hare snitched on his partner and was released, while

Burke took the blame and was sentenced to death. What awaited him after his hanging was much worse than even he could imagine.

The tables were turned on Burke, and his body was privately dissected at the University of Edinburgh, which was the same place to which he handed over his victims. A mob of several hundred people gathered outside the surgeons' window to catch a glimpse of the murderer being chopped up.

WILLIAM BURKE

At the time, the dissection was seen as a further punishment for Burke's crimes, and as a form of justice that fitted the horrific

WILLIAM HARE

nature of the murders themselves. As part of the process, the top of his skull was cut off, and his brain was sliced and inspected. Burke's skeleton is now on display at the University of Edinburgh's Anatomical Museum, and a small piece of his brain that was donated by one of the anatomists is held in a glass tube at London's Science Museum.

RACKING YOUR BRAINS

Tinkering with the ol' gray matter

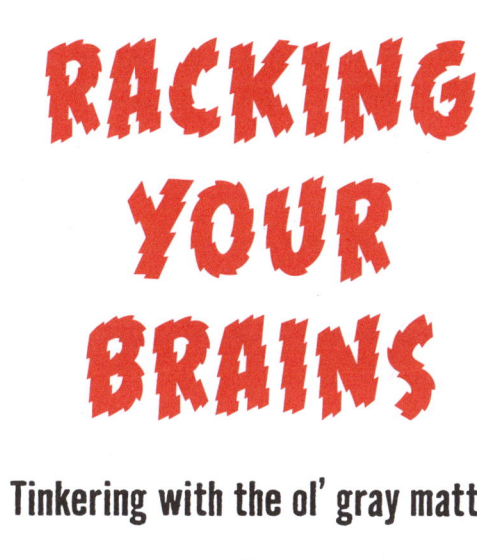

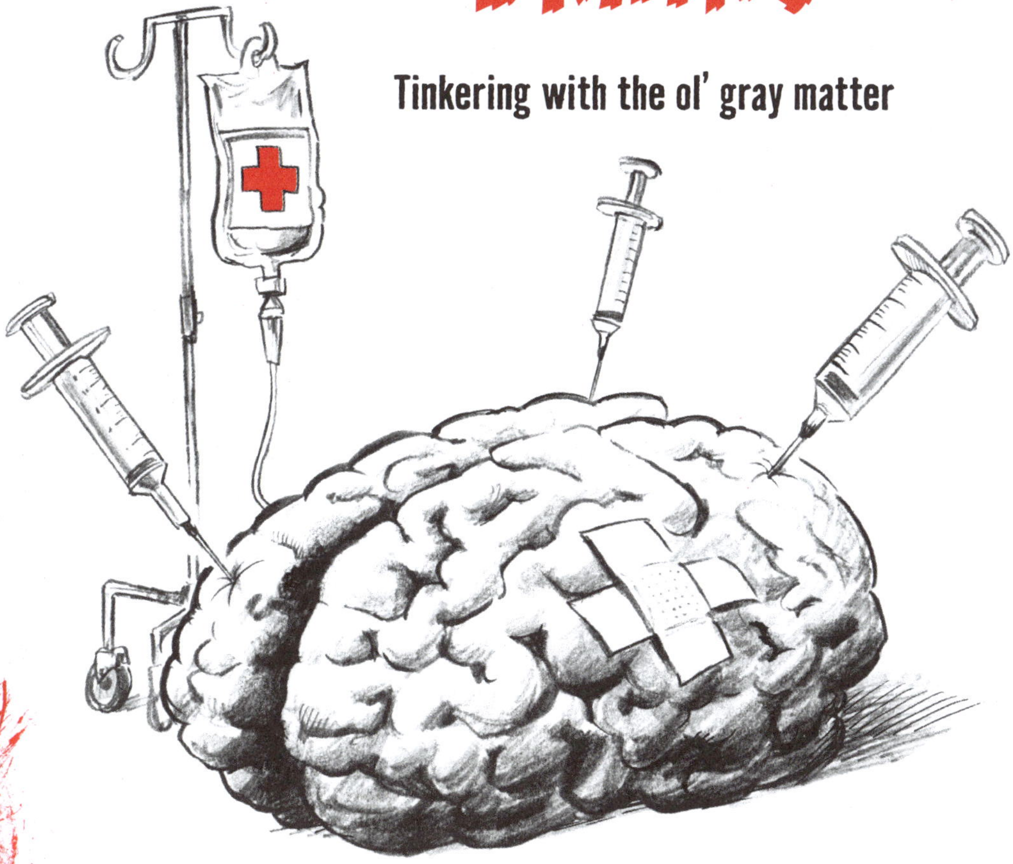

WHILE PEOPLE HAD BEEN DRILLING HOLES into the skull with varying degrees of success for thousands of years, operations on the brain inside it were a totally different matter. It's a super delicate organ, so the risk of damaging it was huge. The brain and its workings were mostly a mystery. But a freak accident in the mid-nineteenth century led to an unexpected slew of discoveries.

In 1848, a railroad worker named Phineas Gage was using an iron rod to pack explosive powder into a hole drilled in the ground. Suddenly, the powder detonated. The rod—which was forty-three inches long and weighed more than thirteen pounds—shot skyward. As it did, it ripped through Phineas's cheek and into his brain, exiting through the back of his skull. The rod, which was smeared with brain matter, landed some eighty feet away.

PHINEAS GAGE

Phineas was thrown onto his back with the force of the blow. But within minutes, he was back on his feet and able to speak—much to everyone's surprise! His coworkers placed him into a cart and took him to the nearest town, where Dr. Edward H. Williams examined him. The doctor noted that he could see the brain pulsating through the opening in Phineas's skull, which he likened to a funnel. At one point, Phineas leaned over to puke, and about a teacupful of his brain fell onto the floor from the hole in his head.

Eventually, another doctor, John Martyn Harlow, took over Phineas's care. He moved him into his own house so he could keep a close eye on him. The road to recovery was long, and there were times when John thought his patient might die. But Phineas did eventually regain his strength. John noted that Phineas knew how much time had passed since the accident and remembered clearly how it had happened. But he struggled with other tasks—like counting money. Within a month, Phineas was able to leave the doctor's house. But something had changed in him.

After the accident, Phineas's friends and family noticed that he was cranky and moody, and prone to outbursts of anger. The railroad-construction company that employed Phineas had considered him a model employee before the accident, but it refused to take him back afterward because of the big changes to his personality. Jobless and depressed, Phineas began traveling, and even appeared as a curiosity in P. T. Barnum's famous circus in order to earn money. Twelve years after his accident, Phineas died from a series of seizures that were likely related to his old injury.

Phineas's death did not spell the end of the fascination with his case. Years after he died, poor Phineas was dug up and his skull

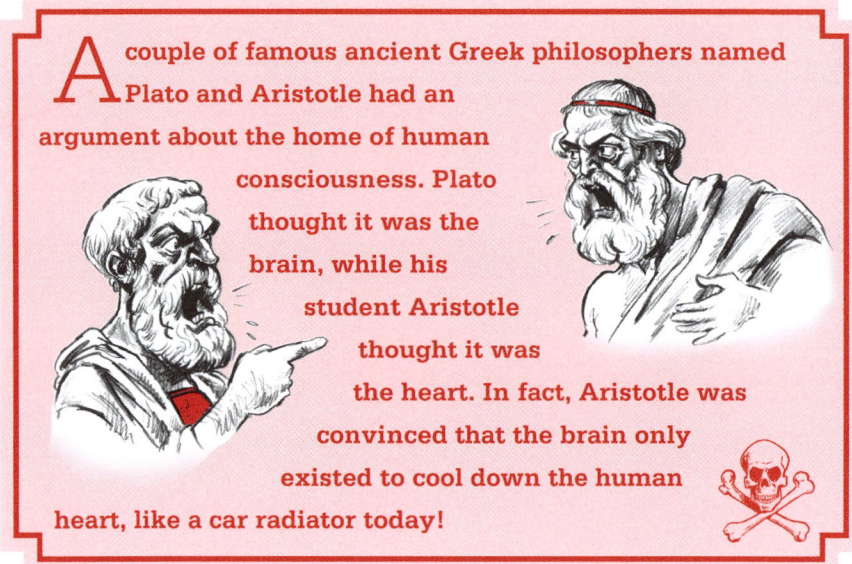

A couple of famous ancient Greek philosophers named Plato and Aristotle had an argument about the home of human consciousness. Plato thought it was the brain, while his student Aristotle thought it was the heart. In fact, Aristotle was convinced that the brain only existed to cool down the human heart, like a car radiator today!

was removed from the body in order to study his injuries. The skull was never returned to Phineas's grave, though, and it's now on display, along with the iron rod from his accident, at the Warren Anatomical Museum at Harvard University.

Phineas had a miserable life, and was treated poorly by modern standards. But his injury, while terrible, did teach doctors that particular areas of the brain are in charge of certain functions, and it helped show them that there's a link between the brain and personality. Weirdly, this was not the last time that a railroad accident would lead to a breakthrough in our understanding of the brain.

A little earlier in the nineteenth century, when rail travel was first invented, there was a lot of worry about how the blistering speeds of locomotives might damage the body. After all, twenty-eight miles per hour was pretty mind-blowing in 1829!

As well as fearing railroad crashes, some folks were seriously concerned that going faster than the average horse would squash their internal organs against the backs of their rib cages, or that women's wombs might even fly out of their bodies! And in Britain, there was a widespread belief that the increasing speeds, and the vibrations they caused, were leading to brain damage.

There were certainly some strange things going on with people who had been involved in railroad accidents. Oddly, some of

Engineer Robert Stephenson's "Locomotion No. 1" was the first steam-powered locomotive to carry passengers on a public railroad. In July 1828, the boiler of the train exploded in County Durham, England, killing the driver. In 1829, Robert built his most famous locomotive, "Rocket." British statesman William Huskisson became the world's first bystander to be killed by a train when he was run over by the Rocket, which was traveling at twenty miles per hour. Present was the Duke of Wellington, who hated the whole idea of railways because he thought they would encourage common people to move about.

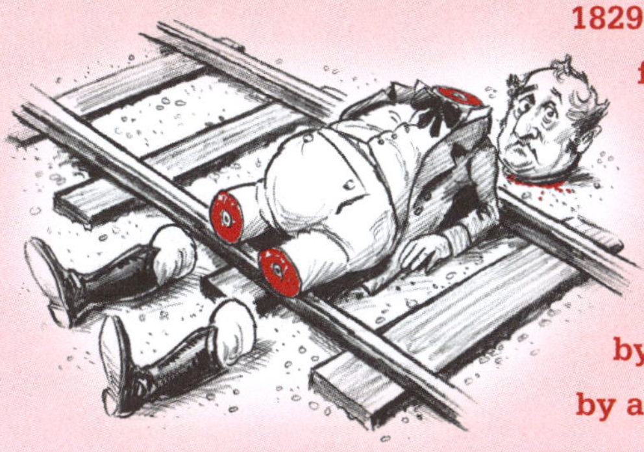

them who appeared unharmed began suffering confusing physical symptoms. These included headaches, memory loss, bladder problems, back pain, and sleeplessness. A few people even lost the use of their legs.

In a lot of cases, the symptoms lasted for years, and doctors were at a loss to explain them. Most doctors thought these symptoms were all nonsense dreamed up by phonies or wimps, and that women, in particular, were most likely to make up such problems because they were weak-willed! And the railroad companies thought they were all just fakers who were looking for a payout. Medical science at the time just didn't know enough to get to the bottom of it.

A surgeon named John Eric Erichsen looked into the problem and put forth the idea that what he called "spinal concussion" was to blame. Today, we use the word "concussion" to describe the damage caused to the brain when it bashes against the inside of

the skull. Concussions can happen as the head is jerked back and forth on top of the backbone in a sudden crash. We refer to this jerking effect as whiplash. But back in John's day, the public and press called it "railway spine."

While concussions from whiplash offered a logical explanation for the symptoms suffered by people *involved* in railroad accidents, the weirdest thing was that "railway spine" symptoms could also be felt by those who merely *witnessed* an accident. Neither John nor any other doctor could offer any reliable explanation for this strange condition in the nineteenth century. The invisible nature of the damage to the brain made it impossible for doctors to understand it. It took medicine a very long time to figure out what was going on with these bystanders.

It wasn't until the 1980s that it was given its modern name: post-traumatic stress disorder (PTSD). This happens when people experience or witness something distressing. This could be a war, a murder, or even a railroad crash. Going through severely upsetting and overwhelming experiences can rewire the brain, causing physical and mental symptoms. Although this medical mystery took more than a century to solve, John's work on "railway spine" is often credited as one of the first major attempts at defining PTSD, and it sparked a global effort to understand it.

While some doctors were focusing on accidental injuries *to* the brain, others were focusing on diseases *of* the brain. In 1884, a young man named Henderson (his first name wasn't recorded) was admitted to a London hospital. Three years earlier, the muscles on the left side of his face had begun to twitch uncontrollably. These attacks became more and more frequent until they turned into full-blown convulsions, during which Henderson would black out. He also lost the use of his left arm. By the time he reached the hospital, he was suffering from really awful headaches, too.

Luckily for Henderson, a Scottish researcher named David Ferrier had published a book eight years earlier on the functions of the brain. In it, he described a series of experiments that he had done on living animals, using electric shocks, to prove that certain areas of the brain were in charge of particular movements of the body. From this work, he drew up a map that showed which parts of the brain controlled which functions of the body. Put simply, David was trying to make the invisible visible!

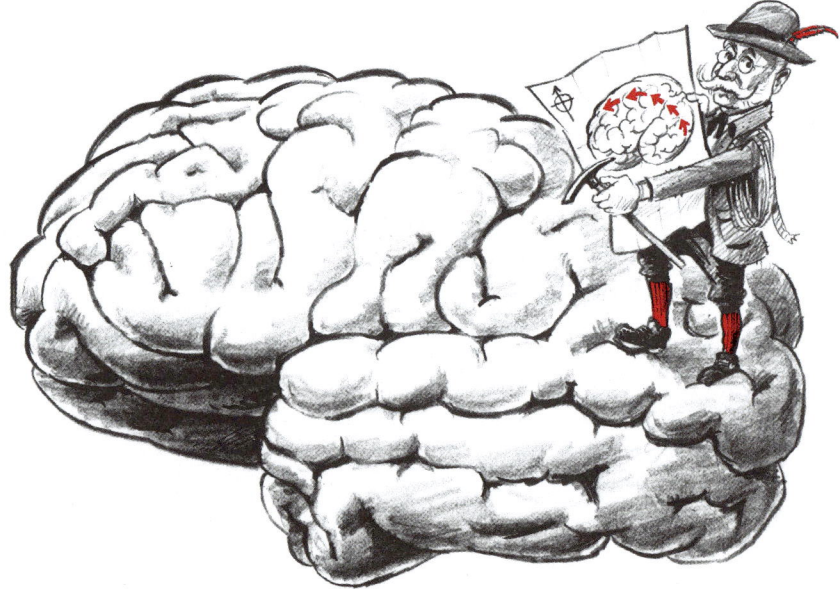

But back to 1884. When Henderson was admitted to the hospital, he was examined by a doctor named Alexander Hughes

Bennett, who just happened to be friends with David Ferrier—a happy accident! Alexander noticed the strange twitches on the left side of Henderson's face, and the weakness in his left leg and hand. Using David's brain map, Alexander realized that Henderson had a brain tumor sitting a few inches above his right ear. Although Alexander believed the tumor to be small, he knew it would continue to grow. Despite the big risks, the only solution was to operate.

The surgeon Rickman Godlee stepped up to the plate. He was the nephew of the great Joseph Lister, the surgeon who became famous for convincing the world of the existence of germs. Rickman was big on following his uncle's surgical rules for lessening the risk of infection. Everyone agreed he was the right man for this job.

Alexander drew up a diagram that showed the location of the tumor.

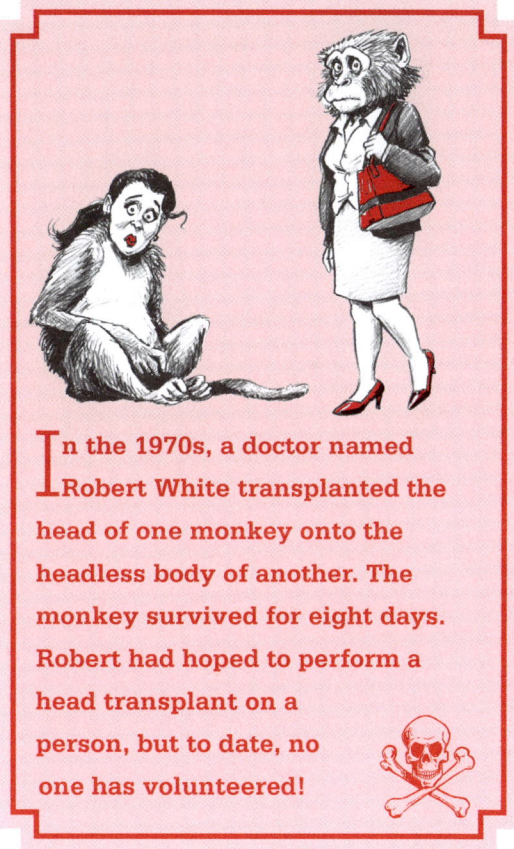

In the 1970s, a doctor named Robert White transplanted the head of one monkey onto the headless body of another. The monkey survived for eight days. Robert had hoped to perform a head transplant on a person, but to date, no one has volunteered!

Henderson was anesthetized with the drug chloroform. And then, Rickman opened up Henderson's skull. At first, Henderson's brain appeared normal and healthy, and Rickman worried that his colleague had gotten the location of the tumor wrong. But after Rickman made a small cut into the brain, he found the tumor lying just below the surface—exactly where Alexander had predicted it would be! Using his finger and a metal spatula, Rickman carefully removed the walnut-sized tumor from Henderson's head.

When Henderson awoke, he said that his headaches were gone. But Rickman's success was short-lived. Although he had followed his uncle's hygiene rules in the operating theater, his patient still went down with an infection. Two days before Christmas, Henderson died.

Nevertheless, the case excited other doctors. It was the first time that a brain tumor had been located through its symptoms alone. Plus, it was the first time that a growth had been removed from a patient's brain. And it had been made possible by the work of David Ferrier. He had been inspired by the case of our old pal, the railroad accident victim Phineas Gage, who was the first to provide a "window" into the brain and its workings. Indeed, had it not been for Ferrier's work, Phineas's story may have been lost to the ages.

A TASTE OF THEIR
OWN MEDICINE . . .

The eighteenth-century Connecticut doctor Elisha Perkins was the inventor of the Perkins Metallic Tractors. They might sound like farming equipment, but they were actually a simple pair of short metal rods, and Elisha claimed that by touching them to the skin, they could draw out many diseases, including rheumatism, epilepsy, inflammation, and disorders of the face.

These rods became the talk of the nation, and Elisha journeyed to Philadelphia to give public demonstrations of them. They got members of Congress very excited, and sold like hot cakes. Even George Washington bought a pair. Elisha began marketing his tractors in Europe, where his son hawked them to the public. A Perkins Institute was set up in London, with an English lord as its president.

Meanwhile, Elisha was looking at ways to treat a nasty disease called yellow fever that was running wild in several cities. He came up with a medicine that he claimed could cure the sickness, although it was really not much more than vinegar. When he took it to New York, it was shown to be useless, and Elisha did his reputation even more damage by dying of yellow fever himself in 1799. Eventually, his tractors were mocked by doctors, the public, the press, and the cartoonists of the time.

But some good did come out of all this nonsense . . .

Some English doctors carried out experiments with Elisha's invention. They found that they could use rods made of any material, and as long as patients thought they were being treated with genuine Elisha Perkins tractors, they did feel better afterward. This was probably some of the earliest research into what's now called the "placebo effect," which means that people can feel better from a treatment, whether it's real or not, simply because they believe it works. Placebo research gave us an important insight into how the human brain functions.

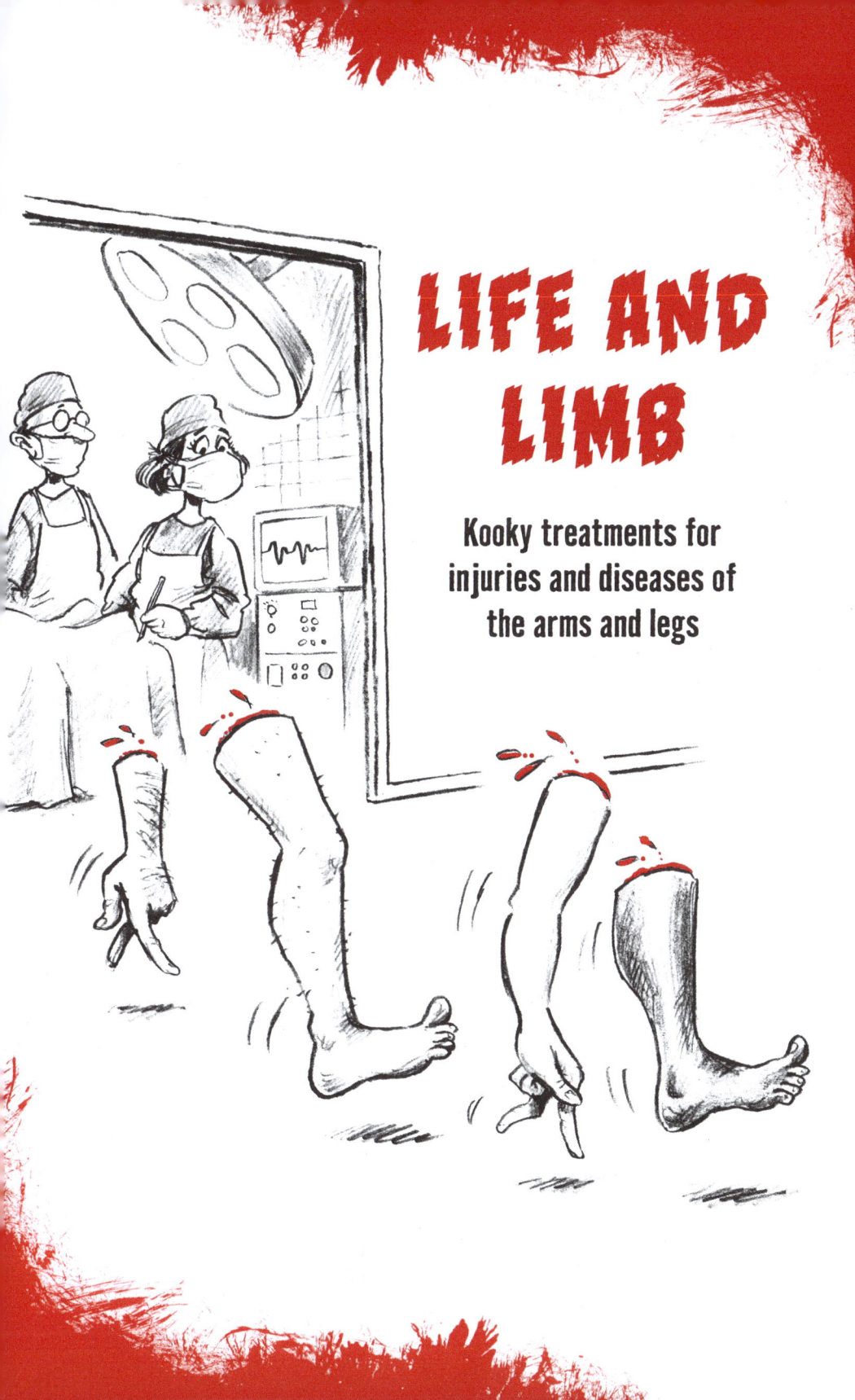

LIFE AND LIMB

Kooky treatments for injuries and diseases of the arms and legs

KING CHARLES II OF Navarre was known as "Charles the Bad," and in an age full of really nasty rulers, this was quite an achievement. In fact, when he fell seriously ill in 1387 and lost the use of his arms and legs, it was blamed on his wicked ways. Doctors were called to his palace in Pamplona in northern Spain, and they ordered a remedy for him that involved being wrapped in cloth soaked in strong booze. So far, so peculiar.

Things got seriously bad for the Bad, though, when a serving woman was told to sew him into the wrappings at night. After she'd done so, there was a length of thread hanging from the stitching, but instead of trimming it, she decided to singe it off with a candle. When the flame touched the booze-drenched cloth, the king was set alight like a barbecue on the Fourth of July, and he was horribly burned. The servant ran off, and Charles eventually died after two weeks of agony.

Even without the unplanned bonfire, it's pretty obvious that the liquor body-wrap technique would have had zero effect on Charles's paralyzed limbs, whatever had caused the problem. But doctors of that age, and of ages to come, were full of similarly bizarre ideas on how best to deal with ailments and injuries of the arms and legs.

A little over a hundred years after Charles the Bad was burned to a crisp, a popular character called "Wound Man" was created. He might sound like the worst superhero ever, but he was actually a medical illustration that first appeared in a book about surgery in 1491.

In a dangerous age, Wound Man was the central figure in diagrams that showed many of the injuries someone might suffer on the battlefield or in accidents. These also showed some outward signs of disease, and a few bites from venomous animals. Wound

Man is usually drawn as a standing figure with knives, swords, clubs, axes, cannon-balls, and thorns damaging or sticking out of every part of his body. He's often surrounded with notes suggesting treatments for these injuries. The problem was, though, that for much of history, many of these treatments were useless at best, and downright dangerous at their worst.

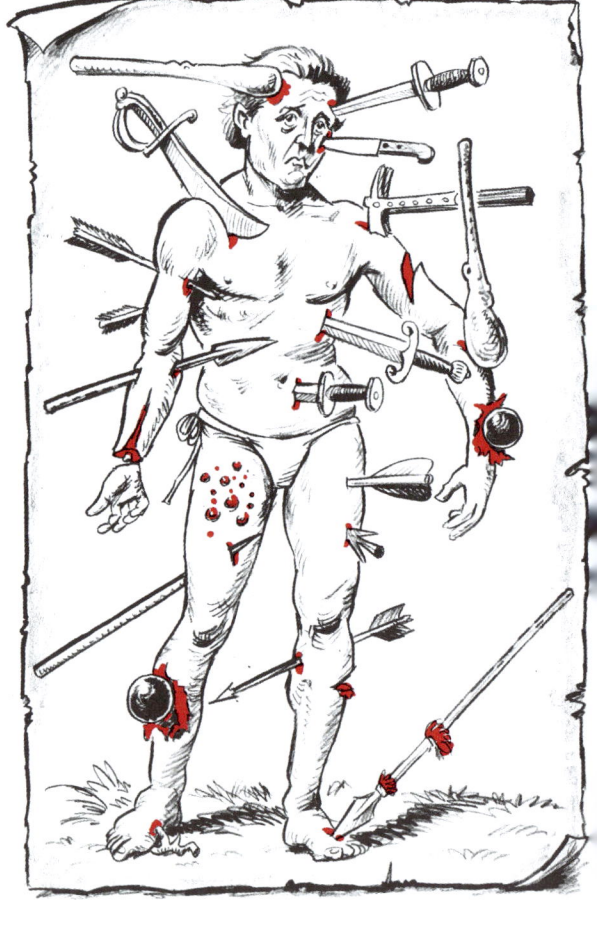

To help explain why this was so, we'd like to introduce you to a really influential and famous Greek doctor named Galen, who worked around 200 CE in the days of the Roman Empire. In fact, he became the personal doctor of the Roman emperor himself, and he pioneered some cool stuff, like early eye operations.

Now, Galen was a super smart guy who got a bunch of things right much of the time. As a young man, he was appointed doctor to a school of gladiators. This allowed him to learn a lot about how to treat wounds—which he called "windows into the body"—since the gladiators fought each other in armed combat in the arena and often got hurt. One of his successful treatments involved using wine to prevent wounds from becoming infected. This worked because the alcohol killed the bacteria, but nobody, including Galen, would understand this for centuries to come.

But Galen got as much wrong as he got right. A lot of his mistakes happened because the laws of the time prevented him from dissecting dead humans. Therefore, he could only learn anatomy from dissecting dead animals—which led to many blunders. For instance, he based his description of a human womb on the womb of a dog!

Nevertheless, Galen's great success as a doctor meant that those who came after him often failed to challenge his views, some of which were downright wrong because of the limitations he faced. This went on for many centuries. Indeed, some of Wound Man's treatments were based on Galen's incorrect ideas about the human body. As a result, medical knowledge in Europe pretty much came to a standstill.

In seventeenth-century Europe, there was a useless wound treatment called the "Powder of Sympathy." But it wasn't applied to the wounds themselves. You were meant to rub it onto the weapon that had caused an injury! Apparently, you didn't have to be in the same room, or even the same country, as the patient. As long as you had the offending weapon, you could heal the wound from a distance. In 1627, a writer recorded that the powder's ingredients could include moss from a dead man's skull, and fat from a bear and a boar. One of the powder's big fans was Englishman Sir Kenelm Digby. His 1658 recipe involved grinding up "Roman vitriol" (copper sulfate), running it through a sieve when the sun enters the zodiac sign of Leo, and then drying it in the heat of the day.

The situation began to change in the sixteenth century thanks to the brilliant young professor of medicine named Andreas Vesalius. We met him back when he was trying to patch up the head of Don Carlos of Spain, remember? Anyway, in 1543, Andreas came out with a revolutionary book about anatomy. Unlike Galen, whose understanding of human anatomy was based on what he learned from dissecting dead animals, Andreas was allowed to cut open the bodies of executed murderers. The dissection was ordered by the court as an additional punishment for the person's crimes. It would never be allowed today, of course, but Andreas learned a great deal from studying these bodies.

When Andreas published his book about his work, it was filled with wonderful drawings of the body by skilled artists—which were far more detailed than anything Wound Man had to offer. He gave the world a much better understanding of human anatomy than it had ever had before. He encouraged doctors and scientists to do their own thinking and research, and not to rely so heavily on the ancient "wisdom" of Galen and others. But, as we will soon see, breakthroughs are often slow to come. And for many doctors over many centuries, the "cutting edge" simply meant reaching for a big old blade and getting to work.

For most of human history, limb amputations were extremely risky and often ended in the death of the patient. In the twelfth century, an Arabic writer named Usāmah ibn Munqidh described an amputation by a doctor on a crusading European knight. The doctor examined the knight, who had an ulcer on his leg, and then asked him if he preferred to "live with one leg or die with two?" The knight replied, "One leg." After laying the limb on a block of wood, the doctor beckoned an axe-man over. With two blows, the leg was amputated. Unfortunately, none of them had considered the third possibility of what might happen: the knight died with one limb after staggering blood loss from the amputation.

In spite of such terrible butchery, many injured people agreed to have their limbs hacked off. In 1685, a nine-year-old English boy was hit by a wagon. His leg was crushed under a cartwheel. The limb was so twisted that his heel was stuck in his butt cheek. He remained confined to bed for four long years. When a doctor paid him a visit, the boy begged him to amputate the leg despite the risks. In this case, the doctor was sure the operation would fail, but he agreed to do it as he knew his patient was in great pain. Happily, the boy survived the amputation and went on to live a long life. Despite the high risk of failure, amputations were occasionally successful. This encouraged surgeons to continue seeking improvements. Unfortunately, many of these turned out to be dead ends.

In the early nineteenth century, an English surgeon named William Winchester designed a surgical instrument that looked like something out of a horror movie. He dubbed his invention the "clockwork saw." It resembled a giant pizza cutter with a circular blade and jagged teeth. The saw worked using a winding mechanism that made the blade spin on its own—kind of like a modern-day chainsaw.

Unfortunately, William's clockwork saw was really difficult to control. The blade whizzed around and around, making it hard

to hold. Poor William quickly learned that the clockwork saw was just as likely to take off an assistant's fingers as it was to remove a patient's limb!

Thankfully for William's patients (and his assistants), this terrifying device never made it past the experimental stage. The clockwork saw is now on display at the Hunterian Museum in London—where it reminds visitors that for every invention that succeeds, there are many more that fail.

The clockwork saw was a clumsy machine, but why were surgeons so obsessed with speed in the first place? Well, for a long time, there was no such thing as anesthesia—which is what doctors give to people to put them into a deep sleep so they feel no pain during surgery. Before anesthesia, limbs had to come off as quickly as possible to spare their patients any unnecessary pain, since they'd be fully awake. And you won't be surprised to learn that the road to changing all of this wasn't exactly a straight one.

In 1956, archeologists unearthed the skeleton of an early human known as a Neanderthal, who lived more than fifty thousand years ago in present-day Iraq. During his lifetime, he had suffered a crushing blow to his skull, as well as many bone fractures. Most interesting, however, was the fact that his right arm had been amputated. This is one of the earliest signs of surgery on a living individual. We know that the Neanderthal survived because the arm had healed, but the injury may have caused some paralysis down his right side.

In the late eighteenth century, a brilliant young chemist named Sir Humphry Davy had worked in a laboratory in Bristol, England, alongside a man called Thomas Beddoes. Thomas and a guy named Joseph Priestley had been researching whether several newly discovered gases could be used to treat lung diseases.

Young Humphry Davy's research on gases won him a job at London's newly founded Royal Institution of Great Britain. Then, around 1800, Humphry began experimenting with breathing in nitrous oxide. He was fascinated by how the gas made him feel spaced-out and giggly, and he soon began holding "laughing gas" parties for his celebrity friends. He even wrote poetry while under the influence of the gas, and at one point he was using it three times a day! He thought it gave him access to the inner workings of the brain, and that it could reveal the secrets of the universe.

More important, Humphry also once wrote that he thought the gas could be useful in surgery because it deadened pain. But . . . he totally failed to take the idea any further! In fact, it wasn't until around forty years later, in 1844, that nitrous oxide was first used as an anesthetic, by an American dentist named Horace Wells.

Horace had been to a demonstration of laughing gas, during which the person given the gas jumped off a table and bashed his leg. But he told the audience that he had no memory of doing so, and that it didn't hurt when it happened. This gave Horace an idea.

HUMPHRY DAVY

The next day, Horace experimented on himself by having a tooth extracted while under the influence of nitrous oxide. And it worked! He felt no pain. Horace went on to pull the teeth of twelve patients with the help of laughing gas. He then decided to showcase its use to a medical audience in Boston. The only problem was that the gas wasn't given to the patient properly during the demonstration, and he screamed in pain. The audience booed Horace, and he left Boston in disgrace.

This would have been a dead end for the cause of anesthesia had it not been taken up by one of Horace's students named William T. G. Morton. He had recently learned about another promising drug from a chemist friend: a liquid called ether.

WILLIAM T. G. MORTON

William began experimenting with ether. In October of 1846, he showed people its benefits at a public demonstration at the Massachusetts General Hospital in Boston, during which a tumor was painlessly cut out of a patient's neck while he was under the influence of ether.

William saw the money-making potential of ether, and added a sweet-smelling oil to it in the hope of confusing people over what was in it, and keeping the "recipe" a secret. Then he applied for a patent for it. (A patent is a license that gives an inventor the right to stop other people from making, using, or selling their invention without their permission.) But everyone knew ether was the important ingredient in William's product, and so, in trying to patent it, he ended up spreading the word about its miraculous effects! He died while trying to sue Congress for $100,000 in losses from the failed patent.

One thing was for sure, though: the age of anesthesia had dawned. Yay!

But . . . this success actually made surgery *more* dangerous. Because patients were no longer thrashing around in agony when the blades cut into them, surgeons felt more confident about picking up the knife and going deeper into the body. And because they didn't yet know that germs existed, operating theaters became dirtier than ever as the number of surgeries increased. Surgeons would operate on patient after patient using the same unwashed

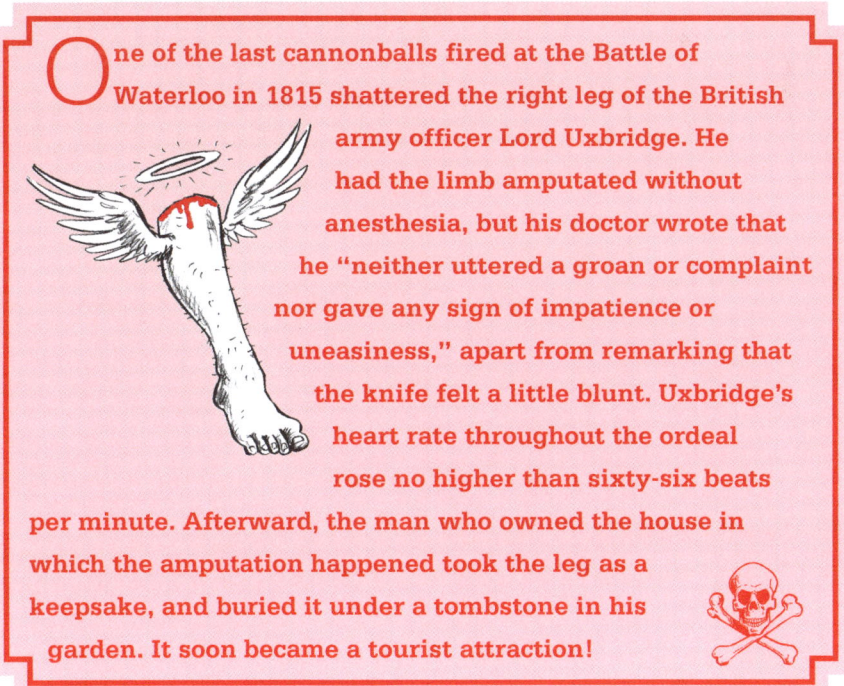

One of the last cannonballs fired at the Battle of Waterloo in 1815 shattered the right leg of the British army officer Lord Uxbridge. He had the limb amputated without anesthesia, but his doctor wrote that he "neither uttered a groan or complaint nor gave any sign of impatience or uneasiness," apart from remarking that the knife felt a little blunt. Uxbridge's heart rate throughout the ordeal rose no higher than sixty-six beats per minute. Afterward, the man who owned the house in which the amputation happened took the leg as a keepsake, and buried it under a tombstone in his garden. It soon became a tourist attraction!

instruments on each occasion. As a result, patients began dying in higher numbers due to high infection rates.

Around this time, our old friend John Eric Erichsen—who championed the idea of "spinal concussion"—wrote that he was convinced surgery had gone as far as it could. How wrong he was! But it wouldn't be until the idea of germs and how to control them was finally and fully understood that things would start to change. John could only see what was in front of his nose, and he wasn't open to new ideas. But openness has been the driving force of change throughout the history of medicine. Germ theory was one of those totally new ideas that took time to gain a foothold. So progress is often accompanied by setbacks.

Improvements in surgery may have made it easier and less painful to remove a limb, but that still left many patients with mobility issues afterward. It's something that doctors have been grappling with for thousands of years.

The earliest example of a prosthesis that we know of isn't a leg, an arm, or even an eyeball. It's a big toe, and it belonged to a noblewoman who lived in Egypt between 1065 and 740 BCE. It was made from wood and leather, and it could even bend at the joint. We know the woman wore it for many years because there's evidence that it was adjusted and refitted for her several times.

Soldiers who lost their limbs during war often used makeshift limbs cobbled together from wood or metal. For example, the Roman general Marcus Sergius Silus lost his right hand in battle, between 218 and 201 BCE. He replaced it with an iron hand that was designed to hold his shield.

We can all agree that war is grim, but it has led to a bunch of medical advances. And sometimes it's patients

who use their voices and their imaginations to drive change. Take James Hanger, for example. He left college to join the Confederate Army during the Civil War. At the beginning of a battle, he ran to

JAMES HANGER

get his horse from a stable and was hit in the leg by ricocheting cannon fire. He was injured horrifically. The bottom half of the leg was hanging by only a ragged piece of skin. Despite the pain, James managed to crawl into the stable's hayloft, but he was still captured by Union soldiers about four hours later.

Infection had already set in by the time that a Union Army

doctor came onto the scene. He acted quickly. He ordered the Union soldiers to break a barn door off its hinges to create a makeshift operating table. He then had two soldiers hold James down while he cut off what was left of his leg, about seven inches above the knee.

James found life after the amputation pretty tough. He hobbled around as a prisoner of war with a crude wooden limb where his leg used to be. After he was released in an exchange of prisoners, he returned home to Virginia. He received a new artificial limb, but it was nothing more than a "peg leg," which was a common prosthetic at this time, fastened by a leather strap around the waist. It wasn't much different from the simple wooden leg you might see on a cartoon pirate. It was painful to wear, and because it didn't bend, James needed crutches or supports to move around.

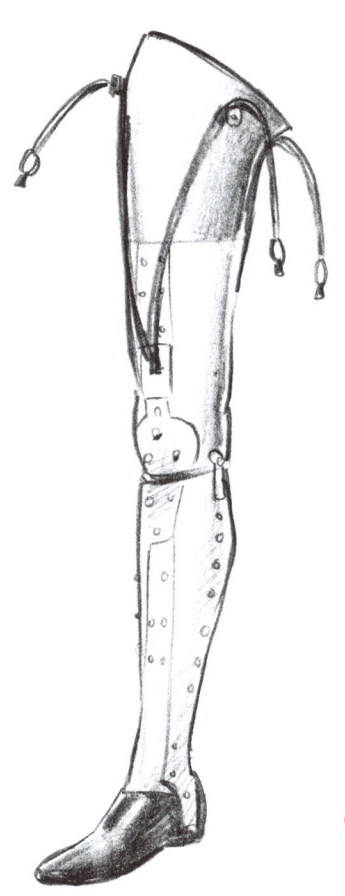

But if medicine had failed to improve his newly difficult circumstances, James was determined to help himself. That was when he began designing his own replacement limb, or "prosthetic."

Eventually known as the "Hanger limb," it was the first prosthetic with fully flexible joints, allowing it to bend at the knee and ankle. This major breakthrough made its wearer far more mobile than the standard-issue peg legs could ever do.

James's design was also the first to use rubber in the ankle and cushioning in the heel, making it a lot more comfortable to wear.

James eventually patented his design, and he started selling his jointed legs to soldiers who'd also had amputations. Within four years, he had already sold over fifty thousand! Losing a limb in the nineteenth century made life very hard for soldiers. Amputation didn't just mean losing your independence. It also made it difficult to find work and provide for yourself and your family. James bettered the lives of countless soldiers because of his invention, and gave them back a sense of worth. Today, Hanger, Inc. is the leading supplier of artificial limbs in the United States, with more than eight hundred locations around the country. Sometimes all it takes is a dash of desperation and a healthy helping of gumption to change the world!

A TASTE OF THEIR OWN MEDICINE . . .

Throughout history, doctors often took the view that just because you're dead, it doesn't mean you can't be useful. In the past, many people believed that dead bodies had special healing powers, and that eating parts of them could cure the sick. Even the great artist and scientist Leonardo da Vinci believed in the powers of "corpse medicine." The bodies of those who had died before their time were believed to be especially powerful.

For instance, it was widely thought that the hand of an executed criminal could cure a bunch of illnesses. As soon as the convict had been pronounced dead, the crowd would rush forward

to touch the hand of the corpse dangling from the noose. Some people also believed that the same hand, if dried, pickled, and holding a candle made from the criminal's own fat, would make the person who carried it invisible. This was known as the "Hand of Glory." And some believed it even had the power to unlock doors.

Nothing was wasted when it came to the corpse of a criminal, and the fat was especially prized. The seventeenth-century surgeon Richard Wiseman once claimed that a woman's swollen legs were cured by being rubbed twice a day with human fat. And in 1736, a woman sold the body of her executed husband to a surgeon for half a guinea, which was a nice chunk of change back then!

BLEEDING HEARTS

Foul-ups to do with the ticker

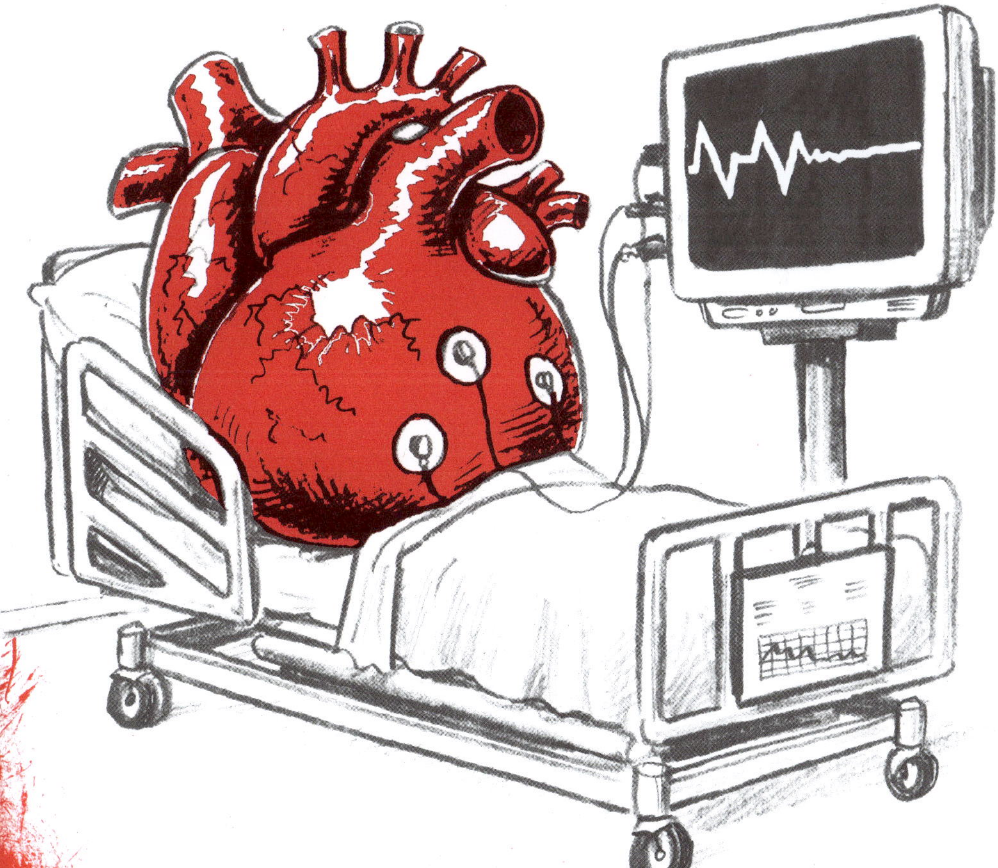

DOING ANYTHING HELPFUL FOR heart problems was super tricky for centuries. This was mostly due to surgeons being unable to operate on this vital organ before anesthesia was invented in the mid-nineteenth century. But sometimes doctors did at least pull out their knives and look at the damaged hearts that had killed their patients. In the fall of 1760, one of those dead patients was the king of Great Britain.

On an October morning, King George II woke early, drank his usual cup of hot chocolate, and then went to sit on his toilet. Shortly afterward, his servant heard a loud pop, and found George stone dead on the floor. It was too late to help the king, but the next day, his doctor cut him open. He later described what had happened to George's main artery, known as the aorta, which carries blood from the heart to the rest

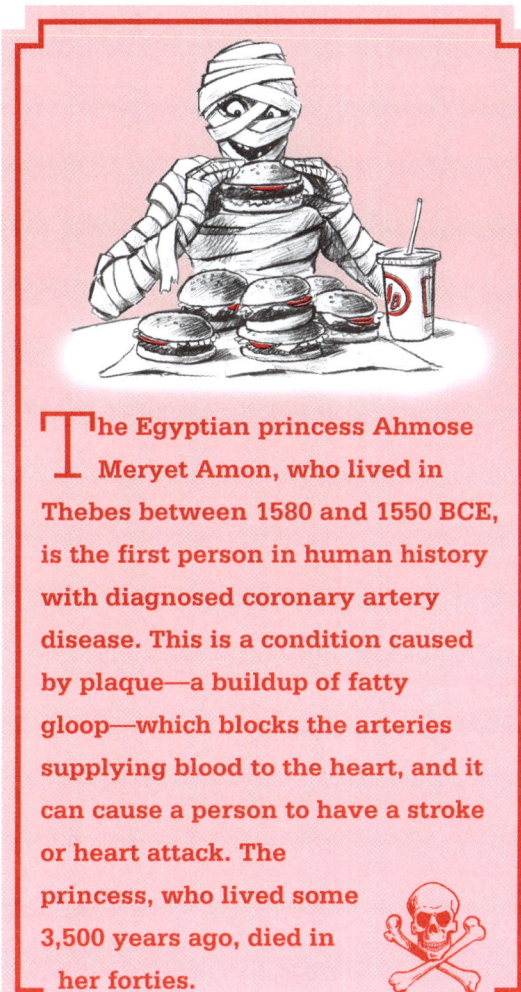

of the body. It had burst open catastrophically, and this explained the noise heard by his servant! Ouch.

Like the brain, the heart is an incredibly delicate organ, and a lot of progress in treating it couldn't be made without serious risk of damage and death. It wasn't until the nineteenth century that there was a big breakthrough in repairing failing hearts. As is so often the case in medical history, this was thanks to a lone doctor who thought he saw a pioneering way ahead. In 1893, a young Chicago man named James Cornish was rushed to Provident Hospital after being stabbed in the chest. This hospital was owned and run by a talented African American surgeon named Daniel Hale Williams.

The Egyptian princess Ahmose Meryet Amon, who lived in Thebes between 1580 and 1550 BCE, is the first person in human history with diagnosed coronary artery disease. This is a condition caused by plaque—a buildup of fatty gloop—which blocks the arteries supplying blood to the heart, and it can cause a person to have a stroke or heart attack. The princess, who lived some 3,500 years ago, died in her forties.

In a small, crowded operating room, Daniel proceeded to

examine the wound. He then cut through the chest wall to create a small window to the heart in order to better see the organ. He noticed there was damage to two of the arteries entering the heart. Daniel held the edges of the wounds with forceps and stitched them back together as James's heart continued to beat.

DANIEL HALE WILLIAMS

James made a full recovery and walked out of Provident Hospital fifty-one days later. He went on to live for another twenty years. As for Daniel, he became known as the first doctor ever to perform open heart surgery successfully. Later, he also became the first African American doctor to be admitted to the American College of Surgeons.

Later attempts to repair wounds of the heart were not so successful. Doctors continued to be scared to operate on this hugely important organ. Those who did give it a shot often hit dead ends. In the 1920s, several surgeons in Boston began blindly inserting scalpels into beating hearts in an attempt to open up the valves that had narrowed due to disease. The results were grim: all the patients died except for one, who did not survive very long either.

Occasionally, a trailblazing loner had a breakthrough, but their surgical colleagues could still find a way to turn these successes into failures. Take, for example, the British surgeon Henry Souttar. In 1925, a fifteen-year-old girl was in his care, and one of her heart valves was too narrow. Henry opened up her chest, and pushed his finger into the valve to explore it and correct the narrowing. This finger technique had never been tried before. Much to Henry's surprise, it worked, and his patient lived for several years afterward. Unfortunately, this was the only time he was allowed to carry out the operation, as his medical colleagues decided it was too risky to try it again. It was twenty-two years before the operation was repeated, after two American surgeons read Henry's account of what he had done.

Henry's operation has been adapted and improved, and is now a routine heart procedure. But it wasn't the only one to have a rocky start.

Treating the heart with electrical machines is now a routine part of medical care, but it took a long time to figure out the best way to put a dangerous force like electricity to good use in medicine.

In 1775, a Danish veterinarian named Peter Abildgaard used electricity to stop and restart the heart of a chicken. This sparked interest in how electricity could be used to influence heart rhythms.

It wasn't long before doctors turned their sights on human subjects . . . whether alive or dead.

As we've already seen with those who did awful things to severed heads during the French Revolution, the rights and wrongs of experimenting on the newly dead were often ignored in the past. The Italian doctor Giovanni Aldini was another guy who saw the bloody work of the guillotine as an opportunity to do science. Giovanni took freshly chopped-off heads and poked electrodes into their brains. This caused the heads to pull faces, with twitching mouths and eyes.

Giovanni became pretty obsessed with his work, and he would later inspire the author of the novel *Frankenstein*, which tells the tale of a driven scientist who brings a monster into being in his laboratory. But far from creating life, Giovanni is best known for his role in an unexpected death.

Giovanni was convinced electrical current could be used for medical purposes. He began by treating people suffering from depression and other mental conditions with shocks to the brain. He also experimented with electricity on the bodies of executed criminals. He even managed to make a corpse's arm lift itself eight inches off the table!

Giovanni toured Europe, thrilling audiences by electrifying human and animal corpses in spectacular shows. He shocked the heads and bodies of horses, sheep, and oxen. He even put the current of a strong battery through a dog's severed head, causing the jaws to open, the teeth to chatter, and the eyes to roll in their sockets. One eyewitness said that it seemed as if the animal was alive again.

Through these experiments, Giovanni believed he was learning how to command the "vital powers," or life force. He was convinced he could use electricity to revive the dead. In 1802, he went to London to wow the medical community and the public with this idea. But to do so, he needed a freshly dead human subject. In January of 1803, one would appear in the shape of George Foster, who was a murderer sentenced to death.

Shortly after being hanged, George's body was cut down from the gallows and taken to Giovanni by a man named Mr. Pass, whose job it was to find corpses for doctors and scientists wishing to perform experiments in this period.

Like a skilled musician playing an instrument, Giovanni touched the electrical rods to various parts of George's corpse in front of spectators who had gathered there to watch the event. *The Newgate Calendar* (a newspaper that covered executions) reported that "the jaws of the deceased criminal began to quiver,

and the adjoining muscles were horribly contorted, and one eye was actually opened." At one point, George's whole body threw itself around to such an extent that some of the astonished spectators genuinely believed he was about to come back to life!

Full disclosure: HE DIDN'T.

Giovanni had certainly amazed the crowd. There was one unexpected turn of events, however. It was reported that "Mr. Pass . . . who was officially present during this experiment, was so alarmed that he died of fright soon after his return home." There's no record of Giovanni Aldini trying to zap any life back into this unfortunate man, though.

By the turn of the twentieth century, cardiac arrests (that's when your heart stops) had become a leading killer in the Western world. Ironically, the condition grew so common because people were getting healthier and living longer, so there was more time and opportunity for their hearts to fail. Once more, people turned their attention to electricity as a possible means of restarting a heart.

There was a turning point in the 1930s, but not thanks to a doctor. It was actually an American electrical engineer named William Kouwenhoven, who cracked the problem when he was given an unusual task. Electricians and linemen—who installed electrical wires so people could have indoor lighting and telephones in their homes—had been dropping dead. And the power company wanted to know what could be done about it.

William performed a series of experiments and found that a

shock delivered to a dog's heart sent the organ into spasm, which is exactly what was happening to those poor linemen who were accidentally touching the electrical wires that they were installing. More important, though, William noticed that a *second* shock (or what he called a "counter-shock") jolted the heart back into a normal rhythm. It seemed that William had pointed the way toward taming the power of electricity and putting it to good use.

His experiments might have led nowhere had they not been picked up by a heart surgeon named Claude Beck, who was working at the University Hospitals of Cleveland at the time. Claude began performing his own experiments on animals. He built a simple machine called a defibrillator that consisted of an electrical transformer, and a variable resistor to control the voltage. Connected to it were two metal tablespoons for delivering the shock to an exposed heart, but with wooden handles to protect the user from being zapped themselves.

Like William, Claude saw that a counter-shock could restore a heart's normal rhythm. But it had never been tried on humans. Would it work?

An opportunity to find out came up in 1947. Claude had been operating on a fourteen-year-old boy when the kid's heart suddenly stopped. Out of desperation, the surgeon ordered some-one to fetch his crude machine from the basement. The first shock failed, so Claude gave the boy a second. That brought him back to life, and the success became national news. Although electricity had produced a lot of dead ends in medical history, it had finally triumphed. Suddenly, we were off to the races!

Nowadays, defibrillators can be found in all kinds of places: doctor's offices, malls, even sports arenas. They are vital to saving people's lives. If someone experiencing cardiac arrest is shocked within the first minute of collapse, the chances of survival are close to 90 percent!

Another common, much smaller heart gizmo only exists today because of a mistake. Pacemakers are devices that use electri-cal impulses to help hearts that are beating too fast, too slow, or irregularly, to beat at a normal rhythm and rate. But when they were first invented, they were HUGE. The earliest one to which a patient was attached was about the size of a piano!

In 1956, an engineer named Wilson Greatbatch was trying to create a machine for recording the sound of a heartbeat. But he accidentally fitted a wrong-sized resistor to his device, and when it was switched on, it started giving out its own beat. He was sur-prised to discover it sounded just like that of a human heart! Could this be put to a different use?

The pulse was a bit irregular, so Wilson tinkered with it, and he was eventually ready to test it out on a dog. Over time, he also managed to shrink it to just two cubic inches. Within a few years, this conveniently sized, fully portable doohickey was implanted in roughly one hundred patients and helped their hearts to beat normally. Today, about 1.7 million pacemakers are implanted every year in people around the world.

Repairing or restarting hearts was one thing, but replacing hearts was a different matter altogether. By now, it won't surprise you to learn that the road to heart transplantation was potholed with setbacks and fear of failure. Progress would require a trailblazing risktaker.

When Boyd Rush was admitted to the University of Mississippi Medical Center with a failing heart in 1964, Dr. James Hardy was waiting for him. James had been experimenting with organ transplantation since the mid-1950s, and he had successfully performed a lung transplant the year before—which we'll get to in another chapter. He wanted to replace Rush's heart with a human equivalent.

Unfortunately, on the day that Boyd was brought to the hospital, no suitable human hearts were available. As the minutes passed, the situation became more and more critical. Boyd was wheeled into the operating theater, where James asked members of his surgical team whether or not he should attempt a transplant using the heart of a chimpanzee.

The surgery went ahead, and several hours later, James and his team made history by performing the first ever heart transplant. The success was short-lived, though. The chimp's heart only beat for ninety minutes inside Boyd's chest before stopping. Unfortunately, it was too small to keep its new human body alive. James's patient died shortly after the operation was complete.

Many medical advances paved the way for doctors to eventually transplant organs. In the early twentieth century, a French surgeon named Alexis Carrel developed a new technique for sewing blood vessels back together. He was inspired by a woman named Marie-Anne Leroudier, who was one of the finest seamstresses in the French city of Lyon. Among many things, she taught him to use tiny little stiches and how to sew with one hand. Alexis practiced his new skill on cigarette paper, which he likened to the fine, papery texture of blood vessels. Thanks to Marie-Anne's coaching, Alexis's technique revolutionized surgery and earned him a Nobel Prize.

One man's failure, however, was another man's inspiration.

In 1967, Christiaan Barnard—a young surgeon in Cape Town, South Africa—was caring for a patient named Louis Washkansky, who was suffering from incurable heart disease. Knowing that without a new heart he would die, Louis agreed to allow his doctor to attempt to replace it with another human heart. The opportunity came one day in early December when a woman named Denise Darvall arrived at the hospital with fatal injuries from a car accident. Her heart was healthy and checked all the boxes that made it suitable for transplantation. The next day, Christiaan prepped his patient for surgery. Over the course of five long hours, he successfully transplanted Denise's heart into Louis's body. There it stayed, beating strongly and steadily for eighteen days, until Louis caught pneumonia and died.

Sure, this wasn't a raving success. But Louis's case was a turning point in the history of medicine. Christiaan later gave a shout-out to James Hardy and the Mississippi team for paving the way for his own work. Over time, improvements made it possible for patients to live longer and longer. Today, thousands of heart transplants are performed each year. And it all began with a failed attempt to transplant the heart of a chimpanzee into a man.

CHRISTIAAN BARNARD

A TASTE OF THEIR OWN MEDICINE . . .

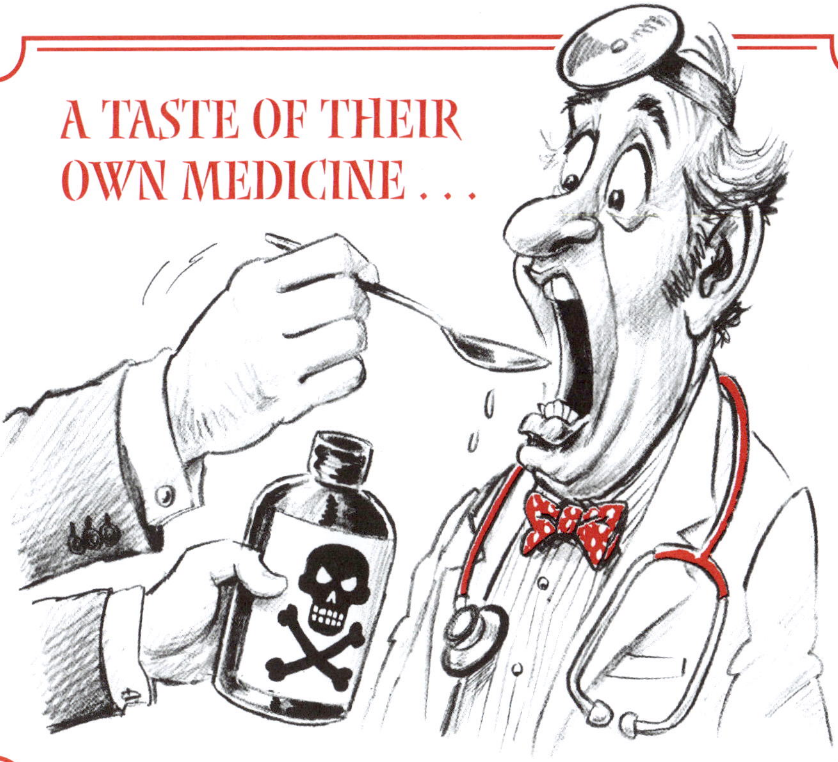

On a wintry evening in 1750, politician and science geek Benjamin Franklin invited some pals over to his house for a dinner party. He wanted to blow their minds with the newly discovered powers of electricity, the exciting possibilities of which were causing such a buzz among scientists and doctors. Benjamin's idea was more about his belly than the good of mankind, though. He planned to electrocute a turkey—which he believed would make the meat of the bird especially tender and tasty.

It wasn't the first time Benjamin had entertained his guests with electricity. A year earlier, he had hosted an elaborate electrical barbecue, during which various meats were roasted by a fire that was kindled using electrified bottles. Guests even drank from electrified glasses that gave them a small shock as they sipped their wine.

But the dinner in 1750 was destined to be a failure. As Benjamin prepared to electrocute the hapless turkey, there was a bright flash and a loud crack. The inventor and statesman had accidentally absorbed the charge, shocking himself senseless! Recalling the event later, Benjamin admitted that he was lucky to have survived the jolt. His pride, however, had suffered a terrible blow.

BAD BLOOD

Doctors who made
a bloody mess
with the stuff
in our veins

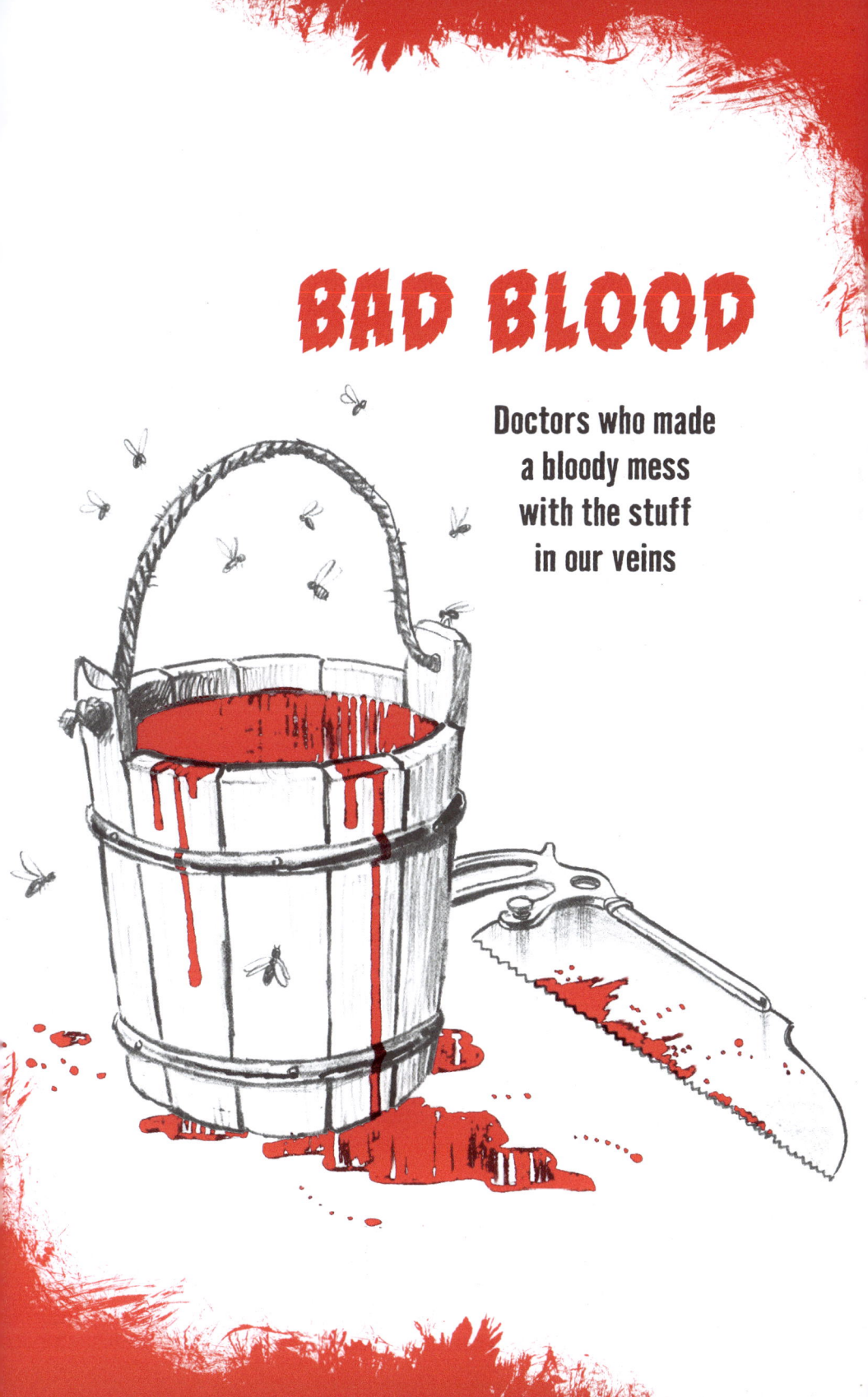

WHEN KING CHARLES II fell ill in 1685, his personal doctor thought he had just the remedy. He quickly slashed open a vein in the king's left arm and filled a basin with his royal blood.

Over the next few days, the British king was tortured by a swarm of doctors buzzing around his bedside. They gave him enemas, which are medicines delivered into the body via the butt. And they urged him to drink various potions—including boiled spirits poured into a human skull. Charles was then bled a second time, before he fell into a coma. He never woke up again.

Even without his doctors' blundering, the king may well have died from whatever was ailing him, but his final days were certainly not made any easier by the endless bleedings.

Bloodletting was a standard part of medical treatment for centuries, requested by many patients in the same way that we might ask for antibiotics when visiting the doctor's office today.

Take America's first president, George Washington. When he awoke one December morning in 1799, he complained of having difficulty breathing. He then asked a member of his staff to bleed him because he was worried his doctor wouldn't arrive in time. The cut was deep, and George lost nearly half a pint of blood. Eventually, a team of doctors arrived and bled him four more times over the next eight hours. By nightfall, he was dead. One of the doctors later admitted that he thought the blood loss was partly to blame for George's end.

The practice of bloodletting began in ancient Egypt more than three thousand years ago. From there, it spread to Greece and much farther beyond. Remember our old friend Galen, doctor to a school of gladiators and a Roman emperor? Some of his biggest ideas had to do with blood, which he thought was the product of food. He claimed that after reaching the stomach, food was turned into liquid, which was then sent to the liver, where it was turned into blood. He also thought that good health depended on a balance of blood and other fluids in the body, known as "humors."

Doctors from the ancient world (and almost everybody who followed them) believed that there were four humors: blood, phlegm, black bile, and yellow bile. When these humors were out of balance (or so the thinking went) a person got sick. For example, Galen believed that the body sometimes made too much blood, which then caused fevers, headaches, and even seizures. The only remedy was to rid the body of the excess blood.

Thanks to hardly anyone having the guts to question the mighty Galen for almost forever, bloodletting persisted for thousands of years, and it was a core practice of medicine. But many doctors believed they were far too important to pick up a knife themselves and slice open a person's veins. Instead, they sent their patients to the barbershop!

In earlier times, barbers provided much more than a simple shave and a haircut. Until the late eighteenth century, barber-surgeons

(as they were often called) offered a variety of services: they lanced abscesses, set broken bones, picked lice from hair, and even pulled out rotten teeth. And one of the barber-surgeon's main duties was bloodletting. But don't worry—that guy with the electric clippers in the mall won't be draining bowls of blood out of you these days.

There were lots of ways to bleed a patient, and not all of them involved using a knife. Sometimes, leeches were recruited to do the deed. A leech is a slug-like critter that can suck several times

The barber's traditional striped pole is a reminder of the long-lived but useless practice of bloodletting. The pole represents the rod that the patient gripped to make their veins bulge, making them easier to slice open. The metal ball at the top symbolizes the basin used to collect the blood. The red-and-white stripes represent the bloody bandages used to bind the wound. Once washed and hung to dry on the rod outside the shop, the bandages would twist in the wind, forming the familiar spiral pattern you can see on modern poles.

its own body weight in blood from another animal . . . or a person. Using one of these little guys for bloodletting, while gross, is a bit safer than cutting open a vein.

The use of leeches in medicine became so common that "leech" became a nickname for a doctor. In fact, during the first half of the nineteenth century, this bloodletting technique became so popular that it led to a "leech craze." Throughout England, women known as "leech collectors" would wade into leech-infested ponds with bare legs in order to attract the slimy bloodsuckers. Once the leeches had drunk their fill, they would fall off, allowing the women to sell them to medical doctors.  Unsurprisingly, leech collectors commonly suffered from headaches as a result of blood loss, and sometimes caught diseases from the leeches.

But why did bloodletting remain so popular for so long?

In 1628, an English doctor named William Harvey was the first to describe the role of the heart in circulating blood throughout the body. A lot of further advances in anatomy and diagnostics followed. But the treatments available couldn't keep up with new understandings of the body. Most doctors believed it was better to do something than to do nothing, and so they stuck to old practices.

That said, by the mid-nineteenth century, bloodletting had largely fallen out of fashion. William Harvey had revolutionized the way doctors understood the blood and heart. And eventually, doctors discovered the role that germs played in causing disease, so hardly anybody believed in the Four Humors stuff anymore. We guess the leeches had to find jobs elsewhere.

While many doctors through history were obsessed with taking blood *out* of the body with leeches and lancets, others were trying hard to put it back *in*. Believe it or not, blood itself was sometimes taken as a medicine!

One of the easiest ways to get human blood was from executed criminals. People often gathered round the chopping block to catch a beheaded person's blood as it spurted from their neck. People believed drinking this blood could cure all kinds of ailments, including epilepsy, which we know now is a brain disorder that causes seizures. In Denmark, the writer of fairy tales Hans Christian Andersen once saw parents forcing their epileptic child to drink the blood of an executed prisoner at the scaffold. So popular was this treatment that executioners had their assistants gather the blood into cups to be sold later to the sick.

The famous sixteenth-century doctor Paracelsus recommended drinking blood as a cure, and one of his followers even suggested taking blood from a living body. For those who preferred their blood cooked, a 1679 recipe describes how to make it into marmalade. Yum!

Apothecaries, who were the pharmacists of their day, carried a range of human products, including one sometimes called "mumia." As you might have guessed from the name, this was made from mummies, which are dried or preserved bodies. One medical text from the seventeenth century said that the best mumia came from the bodies of those who had met with sudden and preferably violent deaths.

The supply of mumia couldn't keep up with the demand, so it was really expensive. Many apothecaries sold cheap imitations that usually came from the corpses of beggars, leprosy sufferers, and plague victims. Incredibly, mumia was sold for medical use as late as 1908.

No doctor today is going to suggest you drink a criminal's blood, or have a spoonful of powdered mummy on your breakfast cereal (at least no doctor any of you should be listening to). But, if you think about it, the use of body parts for medical purposes carries on today in the form of organ transplantation, as well as blood transfusions—as we'll soon see. So, although nobody is

consuming bits of the human body anymore, patients may take parts of another person into themselves during these types of medical procedures, which save millions of lives each year.

Actually, the history of blood transfusions is full of dead ends. And much of the interest in the practice began because people thought that pumping fresh blood into someone could make them young again. But more about this later.

Getting blood into someone's veins wasn't possible until the invention of the hypodermic needle. In the eleventh-century CE, the Iraqi physician Ammar ibn Ali al-Mawsili described removing cataracts from eyes using a thin, hollow metal tube. But it wasn't until the seventeenth century that such an instrument was used to inject substances into the body.

In the 1650s, the famous British architect Sir Christopher Wren conducted a series of weird medical experiments to understand if substances injected into the veins would have the same effect as those that were swallowed. He set about creating a syringe from an animal bladder and the sharpened quill of a goose. He then used this syringe to inject wine into his dog's veins!

Christopher's success in getting his dog drunk in the strangest manner possible paved the way for future experiments—most of which were dangerous, if not downright deadly. In 1667, the French physician Jean-Baptiste Denis transfused blood from a lamb into a feverish young man. He figured that because both animal and human blood were red, then they must be identical to each other. Spoiler alert: they absolutely are not! Fortunately, the young man survived, probably due to the small amount of lamb's blood he was given. But Jean-Baptiste's patients were not always so lucky when it came to his blood transfusion experiments.

Not long after his first success, Jean-Baptiste turned his sights on a mentally ill man named Antoine Mauroy. Jean-Baptiste wondered if he could treat Antoine by replacing his "bad" blood with "good" blood. So, he set out to do just that. Over the course of several months, Jean-Baptiste injected blood from a calf into Antoine until he eventually died.

Heartbroken and angry, Antoine's wife accused Jean-Baptiste of murdering her husband. Jean-Baptiste was put on trial, during which he pointed the finger back at Antoine's wife, accusing her of killing her husband with a poison called arsenic. Eventually, Jean-Baptiste was found not guilty, but the French courts outlawed animal-to-human blood transfusions. They feared it went

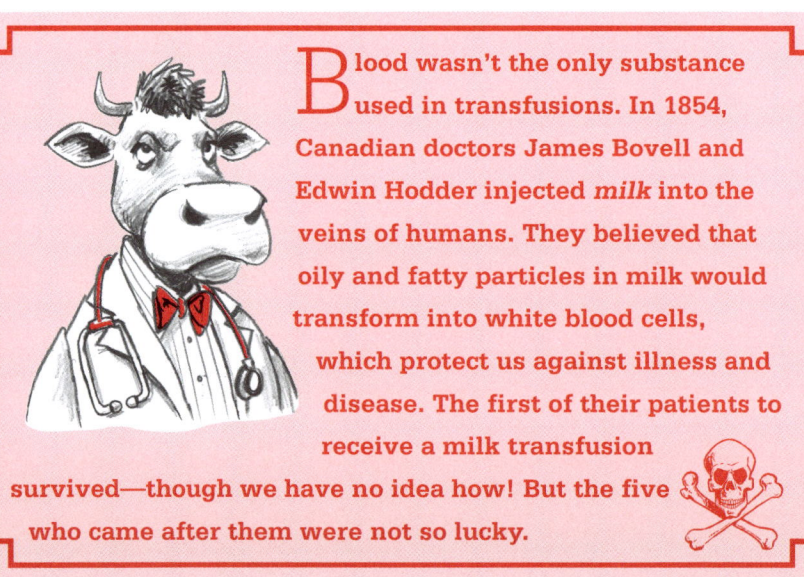

Blood wasn't the only substance used in transfusions. In 1854, Canadian doctors James Bovell and Edwin Hodder injected *milk* into the veins of humans. They believed that oily and fatty particles in milk would transform into white blood cells, which protect us against illness and disease. The first of their patients to receive a milk transfusion survived—though we have no idea how! But the five who came after them were not so lucky.

against nature, and that people might develop horrible side effects, like sprouting horns.

In the eighteenth century, an Irishman called Richard Pockrich suggested that human-to-human transfusions would be a great way of making the old and the sick feel young and healthy again. In fact, he felt sure this could help people live forever. He thought that the perkiest servants in your household could be among those supplying the blood (but only to those rich enough to have servants, presumably).

It wasn't until the nineteenth century that the first human-to-human blood transfusions were actually carried out, by an English doctor named James Blundell. He noted that many of his patients "suffered fever, backache, headache, and passed dark urine" after receiving blood from another person. Many of his patients died, and James couldn't explain this.

Public interest in blood transfusions grew with the publication of *Dracula* (1897), a famous novel by the author Bram Stoker. Bram may have learned about transfusions from one of his three brothers, who were doctors. When one of the book's characters has her blood sucked out regularly by the thirsty vampire, four of the men in the story try to save her life by giving her their blood. But when *Dracula* was published in 1897, everyone had failed to grasp the fact that you couldn't just pump anybody's blood into whoever you liked without some serious risks. Life-threatening reactions to transfusions were common and poorly understood.

In 1900—just three years after the publication of *Dracula*—the puzzle was finally solved by an Austrian doctor named Karl Landsteiner, who won the Noble Prize for his work. For decades,

doctors had noticed that when blood from different donors was mixed, the cells sometimes clumped together. This made the blood thick and sticky, which meant it couldn't freely flow through the arteries and veins. Most doctors shrugged off this strange occurrence or blamed it on the fact that the blood in question often came from sick patients.

Karl had a different idea, though. He began taking blood from healthy people and mixing the samples together. He, too, observed the weird clumping problem. So, he began sorting the samples into groups, which we now call A, B, O, and AB. He noticed when he mixed A with A, there was no clumping. But when he mixed A with B, it clumped. He realized that for the most part, only groups of the same type could be mixed together without clumping. The real oddball was group O, which seemed to mix with all groups without any problem. There were still hurdles to be cleared when it came to blood transfusions, but Karl's discovery made the procedure much safer. To help doctors out, everyone today is tested at birth and assigned a blood group. Do you know yours?

As we hope we've shown by now, medical progress often takes two steps forward and one step back—and this is totally normal. In the case of blood donation, making transfusions safe, and even figuring out exactly what transfusions were good for, was a long and difficult process.

KARL LANDSTEINER

But in one way, medicine has kind of come full circle. Although doctors today aren't draining blood out of their patients because they think it's going to put their Four Humors back in balance, bloodletting has made a bit of a comeback. It can be used as a treatment for certain blood disorders, as a means of managing symptoms and preventing further problems, like liver damage.

The leech has also made a comeback in the twenty-first

century! In certain really delicate surgeries, such as skin grafts, or the reattachment of body parts, sometimes tiny veins struggle to carry blood away from the site of the surgery. So, the blood builds up in stagnant little pools, and can cause the death of the tissue at the site. Very bad news.

But this is when the leeches save the day. Specially bred, disease-free leeches are allowed to latch on to the affected area and suck out the pooled blood. Their spit, or "saliva," really is amazing stuff. Not only does it contain a painkiller—so that the patient can't feel the leeches clamp on with their little mouths—it also contains a chemical that stops blood from clotting and lets it keep flowing, even after they have drunk their fill and been removed. This means the tiny veins have a chance to repair themselves and start working properly.

In 2004, the use of leeches was officially approved in the USA. So the slimy little devils are back on the payroll!

A TASTE OF THEIR OWN MEDICINE . . .

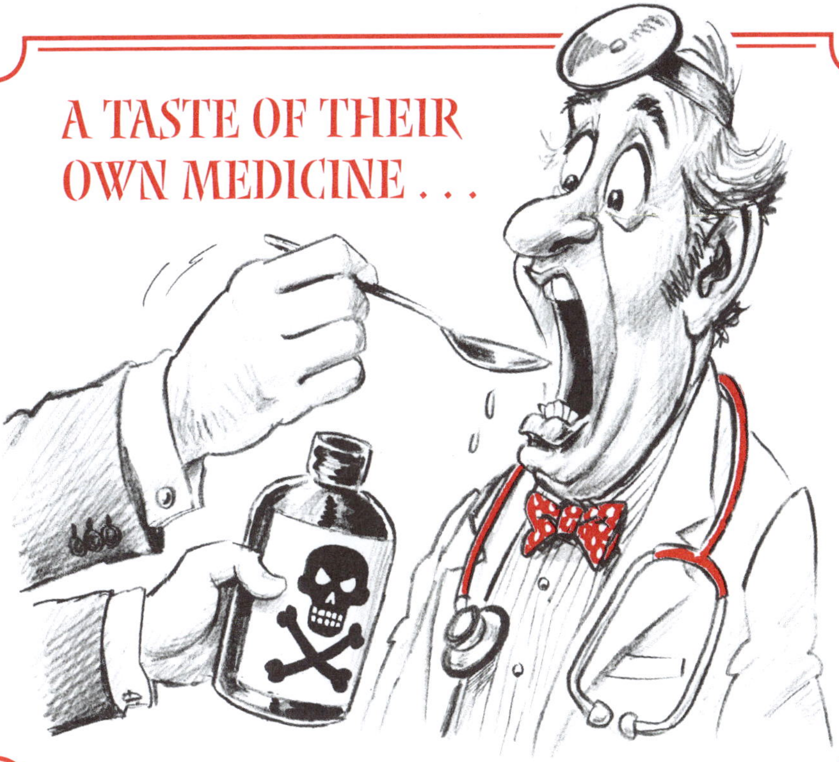

The successful research into blood groups at the start of the twentieth century didn't suddenly make blood transfusions totally safe. Alexander Bogdanov was a Russian doctor and politician, and he was also the founder of the world's first institution devoted entirely to blood transfusion. In 1924, he began experiments with blood in an attempt to live forever.

After performing eleven transfusions on himself, he declared that he had stopped balding and that his eyesight had improved. However, in 1928, Bogdanov became infected with malaria and tuberculosis from a transfusion, and he died shortly afterward. It

turns out that an endless supply of blood didn't make him immortal. In fact, it killed him.

ALEXANDER BOGDANOV

NO GUTS, NO GLORY

Silly ideas to do with digestion, diet, and drinking

WILLIAM BEAUMONT WAS AN army surgeon who worked at a fort in the wilds of Michigan. One day in 1822, a Canadian fur trader named Alexis St. Martin was injured accidentally by a shotgun blast. William was called to help him, and he found Alexis in a pool of blood with a huge hole in his side—big enough for a person's fist to pass through it!

But, amazingly, Alexis didn't die.

William took him in and patched him up as best he could using the techniques of the time. Alexis began to recover and was soon well enough for William to employ him as a handyman. But while the hole in his side shrank, it never fully disappeared.

Surgery's failure, though, was William's scientific—and really *gross*—opportunity. The hole gave him direct access to Alexis's stomach, which had also been punctured by the blast. Looking at the inner workings of the living human body was something doctors were very keen to do for centuries. For most of history, they only really had opportunities to look inside dead bodies. Before the development of modern techniques, like scans and X-rays, it was very tricky to take a peek inside at how our internal organs function. So, William grabbed this chance to learn about exactly what the stomach got up to after food had been shoved into it.

William carried out a lot of experiments on his patient. For instance, he gave Alexis doses of medicine directly through the hole in his stomach. He also hung bits of food on strings in Alexis's

stomach, and then pulled them out again to see how long it took for the food to be digested. He even extracted some of Alexis's stomach acid so he could perform more tests on it outside the body.

Until this point, doctors believed that digestion was entirely a mechanical process. In other words, after the teeth had done their work, swallowed food was mashed into smaller and smaller pieces through a series of stomach contractions. But William's experiments showed that digestion was partly a *chemical* process, and that food was also broken down by an acid and chemicals called "enzymes" inside the stomach. William recorded his findings, which were eventually published in 1833.

A lot like poor old Phineas Gage, who was studied after a metal rod passed through his brain, Alexis became a science project on legs, and he grew understandably sick and tired of it. One day he fled north, back to Canada. He married and had kids, but he was eventually found by William, who paid for Alexis and his family to return to the United States. Alexis ran away a few more times, but William always persuaded him to come back so he could continue

ALEXIS ST. MARTIN

with his experiments, which totaled over two hundred! Eventually, Alexis said that enough was enough, and he called a halt to all the poking and prodding. Incredibly, Alexis outlived William by nearly thirty years, dying at the age of eighty-three.

William Beaumont's experiments, while tough on poor old Alexis, were really important to later scientists who continued the work of understanding digestion.

But a big discovery can always be misunderstood and misused. In other words, science can sometimes find a way of turning a success into a failure. And a lot of history's digestive dead ends were due to determined people spreading what turned out to be misguided, silly, or downright dangerous ideas . . .

When Charles Darwin announced his theory of evolution in 1859, it was like a scientific bomb going off. Charles had explained how all species of living things change over vast periods of time, and this new way of looking at the history of the natural world blew the minds of scientists across the globe.

Decades later, in 1904, an English doctor named Sir William Arbuthnot Lane met the Russian Nobel Prize–winning scientist Élie Metchnikoff. Élie had persuaded himself that human beings were evolving much faster than anyone, including Charles Darwin, had realized. He thought that, as a result, many of our body parts were becoming useless, and would eventually disappear.

Élie thought the colon was one such body part. This is the largest section of your bowels, which leads to your butthole. Élie claimed that colons should be removed, and as a surgeon who had worked hard on new techniques in this area, Sir William agreed with him. As a result, he started removing the colons of some of his patients who were suffering with constipation—which is an inability to poop.

The problem was that there was no real scientific basis for William to be doing this. The colon is, in fact, essential, helping to rid the body of waste after it has digested food. But, throughout history, some people become obsessed with the idea that one simple remedy they have invented is the cure for all known ills.

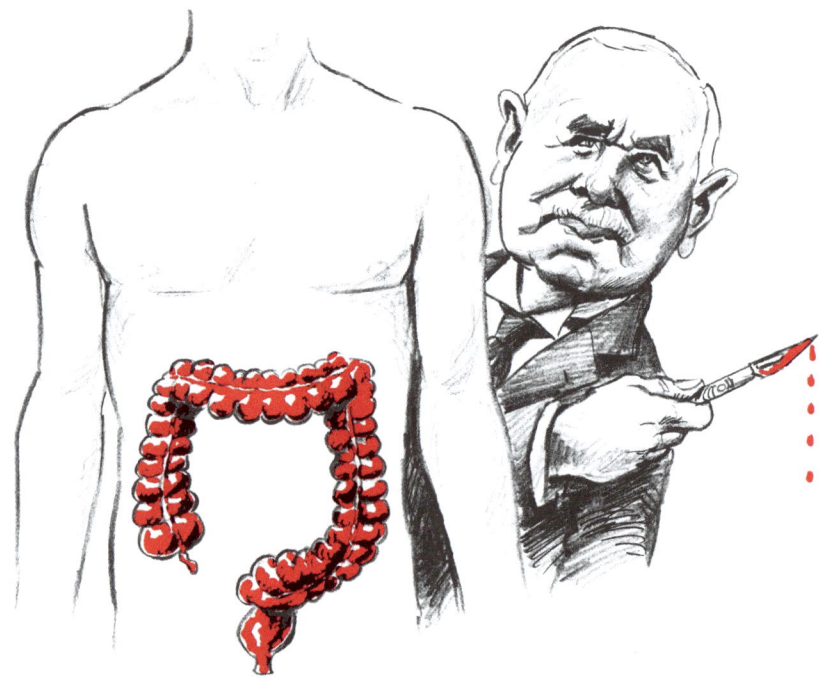

Unfortunately, for William's patients, the realization that the colon was a vital organ came too late.

In 1913, a group of William's medical colleagues attacked him publicly for his beliefs and practices around the colon. However, he was able to rescue some of his reputation by doing a whole lot of good for the soldiers of World War I. Many men suffered terrible facial wounds on the battlefield, and so William helped a pioneering surgeon named Sir Harold Gillies to set up a hospital that came up with brilliant new plastic surgery techniques to repair the damage. William's career was marked by at least this one great triumph, but hacking out people's colons really didn't help him get to the, er, bottom of anything.

We've learned a lot more about how the digestive system works since the days of Sir William Arbuthnot Lane. Arguments over diet, however, have raged for thousands of years . . . and they're still raging today. But in the past, where could you turn for advice about healthy eating? And how useful would that advice even be?

Back in the days of the Roman Empire, there was a politician called Cato the Elder who seemed to think that cabbage could cure just about anything!

In a book he wrote about farming in around 160 BCE, Cato stated that cabbage is a remedy for indigestion, boils and sores, and dysentery (an infection that causes bloody poops). He also said that it could get rid of warts, and that it could even prevent you getting drunk. And he went further than that, saying that if you boil cabbage in wine and pour the liquid into the ear, it will restore hearing. But his weirdest claim was that bathing babies in the warm pee of anyone who had been eating a lot of cabbage could make them grow up strong! In spite of all of this, cabbages failed to stop Cato's first wife and one of his sons from dying before him. (But he was right to think that cabbage and green veggies in general are good for you.)

So, it seems that human beings have always been looking for what are now known as "superfoods." The thinking has often been that somewhere out there is a single type of vegetable, fruit, nut,

Thanks to Hollywood, we think of gladiators as ripped guys with six-packs and arms like jackhammers. But a gladiators' graveyard, unearthed in Turkey in the 1990s, led to a surprising discovery. When scientists tested their bones, they found that the gladiators' diets caused them to carry a lot of body fat. Their food was high in carbs, low in protein, and mostly vegetarian. They ate so much energy-giving grain that they were nicknamed "barley-men." It's thought that body fat helped them escape bad injuries because it gave them a layer of protection. They could suffer surface wounds, but still fight and put on a good show in the arena.

or whatever that will cure all ills and keep us in peak condition. In truth, though, no single food is going to keep you in perfect condition, and enjoying a varied diet is the healthy way to go. But one very hungry fella from history took the idea of eating a wide range of foods to some pretty wild extremes.

William Buckland was the Dean of Westminster Cathedral, London, as well as an important professor at Oxford University in England. He wrote the first full account of a dinosaur fossil, which he named *Megalosaurus*. He was also a founding member of the Zoological Society of London. Luckily for William, this helped him to pursue his lifelong ambition: to taste every animal on Earth!

This was, to some extent, in line with the Zoological Society's aim of bringing exotic animals into the country to help improve the nation's poor diet. But William's joy in eating new critters grew into an obsession, and it distracted him from the society's original goal. No beast was safe from his enormous appetite. Even William's son Frank became interested in eating unusual beasts. In fact, Frank managed to persuade London Zoo to send both his father and himself pieces of any of the animals that had died there.

One of William's favorite meals was toasted field mice, while

other dishes that he served up at his dinner parties included porpoise, hedgehog, earwigs, puppy, bear, crocodile, snails, ostrich, and panther. William once said that the most revolting thing he ever ate was a helping of bluebottle flies, although moles came a close second.

His finely tuned palate was put to the test in some remarkable ways. Once, he got lost while journeying overnight to London. He jumped off his horse and tasted a handful of the soil at his feet, announcing triumphantly—and correctly—that he was in a place called Uxbridge. On another occasion, William visited a cathedral

with friends, who wondered if a curious damp patch on the floor was in fact the fresh blood of a saint that was appearing miraculously. The doubtful William promptly licked the mystery liquid off the flagstones and correctly identified it as bat pee.

The weirdest of his dining adventures happened while he was visiting the Archbishop of York. Just after dinner had been served, the archbishop brought out a silver snuffbox containing what he claimed was the preserved heart of the French ruler, King Louis XIV. (It was a French tradition dating back to the thirteenth century that the internal organs from a dead king's body be removed, mummified, and placed in different locations away from the corpse.) The shriveled heart was passed around the table, and when it reached William, he snatched it and gobbled it down, declaring, "I have eaten many things, but never the heart of a king."

By 1850, poor old William was showing signs of a mental breakdown. Later, he was placed in an asylum, where he died in 1856. Eating a king's heart must not have offended too many people, as William was given a burial plot in Westminster Abbey—which is a huge honor in Britain, and it was more than was granted to the creatures (and bits of people) that he consumed! His dream of improving the nation's diet by getting the people to eat a host of weird and wonderful creatures had ended in failure.

A foolproof way to lose weight is to eat nothing at all, but no doctor today would promote such a dangerous idea. Unfortunately, it wasn't that long ago that a doctor named Robert Linn suggested

Many British kings and queens loved stuffing themselves. King Henry I died in 1135 after eating too many lampreys (a kind of fish). And the banquet to celebrate the crowning of King George II in 1727 lasted three days! There were 105 dishes, including geese, crabs, cheesecakes, venison pasties, veal, jellies, sausages, fruit, fifty plates of garnishes, and pyramids of sweetmeats. Coronations were usually organized by the Dukes of Norfolk, and the eleventh Duke often devoured four pounds of beef in one sitting. He outdid himself on one occasion by gobbling down an astonishing fifteen steaks.

exactly this. In the 1970s, he created what he called the "Last Chance Diet," because you might try it after all other measures had failed. He recommended eating nothing except his wonder product: Prolinn. But selling this was more about the health of his bank balance than the health of his customers.

Prolinn was a drink made from some really gross stuff that was left over from processing animals in slaughterhouses. It included ingredients with next to *no nutrients* in them, such as ground-up hooves, tendons, bones, and hides. These were all pepped up with artificial flavors and colors, and enzymes were included to help break down the tough animal products. Each serving contained only four hundred calories, less than a quarter of the daily calories a human body needs to survive. Of the few million people who tried the Last Chance Diet, fifty-eight suffered heart attacks.

Prolinn was just one in a long line of fad diets through the ages. A century earlier, arsenic diet pills had been advertised as "miracle cures" that could help with weight loss, in spite of arsenic being a highly dangerous poison. Some doctors also prescribed arsenic as a cure for other conditions including rheumatism, worms, and the morning sickness often experienced by pregnant women.

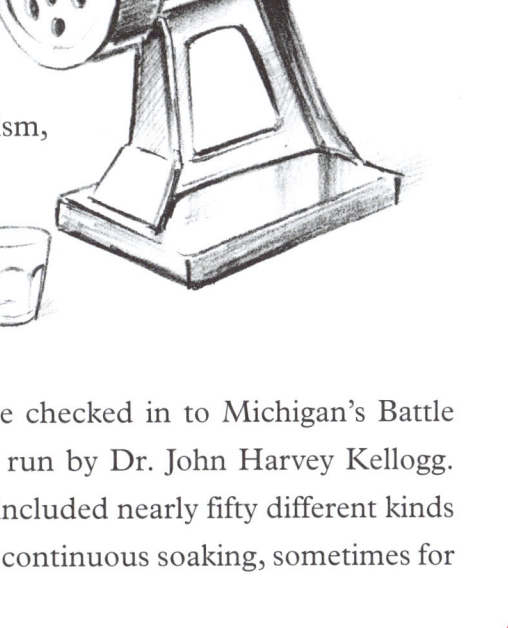

If you were on a health kick at the end of the nineteenth century, you might have checked in to Michigan's Battle Creek Sanatorium, which was run by Dr. John Harvey Kellogg. The range of treatments there included nearly fifty different kinds of baths, one of which involved continuous soaking, sometimes for several weeks.

Dr. Kellogg was a dedicated vegetarian who was also against

JOHN HARVEY KELLOGG

alcohol. A lot like Cato with his cabbages, he thought most ill-nesses, and some problems of behavior, could be cured with a simple diet. He wanted to improve America's digestion and the health of its intestines, and he thought that bland fiber, in the form of whole grains, was the way to go. With this in mind, he created oatmeal and cornmeal biscuits to feed to his patients. Later, he and his brother developed what they considered to be a healthy breakfast for the public: Kellogg's Cornflakes. These quickly became incredibly popular, and they were bought in huge quanti-ties. But while they were a commercial success story, today's nutri-tionists would disagree with the Kellogg brothers about cornflakes

The diet of rich people was very high in meat through much of history, and the importance of eating veggies wasn't properly understood. An English fashion icon named Beau Brummel (1778–1840) was once at a dinner party when another guest noticed he hadn't taken any vegetables. When she asked him if he ever ate any, Beau replied, "Yes, madam, I once ate a pea."

offering any benefits for behavior. And though fiber is good for us, we need more variety in our diet to keep us healthy.

Many of us enjoy a cup of something with our breakfast cereal, and for much of the world, tea is the hot drink of choice. In Britain, tea was first served as a novelty in the busy, gossipy coffeehouses of seventeenth-century London. It was also sold as a medicine in apothecary shops, and soon became an incredibly popular drink. But there were people who believed that tea was actually harming the nation's health. Some even thought that tea could shorten your life by up to fifteen years, and that drinking lots of beer was far better for you!

In 1756, a guy named Jonas Hanway wrote a seriously boring travel book that also contained his strong anti-tea views, and it caused a big public argument. Jonas believed that tea's high cost and the time taken to brew it were negatively affecting the poor and the nation's productivity. He claimed tea caused paralytic and nervous disorders, made women ugly, and caused weak digestion and low spirits. Jonas claimed the poor were spending all their money on tea and not feeding their children, leading to a smaller workforce, and leaving the army short of men in wartime. Jonas urged the rich to give up tea, in the hope that poor people would follow the example of their "betters."

It all sounds like a bunch of scaremongering claptrap. But on the health front, Jonas actually had a point. The quality of the tea that poor people were drinking was often pretty bad. Some dishonest tradesmen were selling tea that wasn't tea at all, because it was made from dried blackthorn leaves. It sometimes contained poisonous substances that made it look like green tea. Some of these fake teas even had sheep poop in them!

Tea proved to be just too darned popular, and Jonas's battle to end tea drinking was a total flop. It's now the most common drink

in the world, apart from a simple glass of water! And today we know that tea is actually good for you.

The human body makes particles called "free radicals." Pumping out too many of these is linked to certain cancers, ulcers, Alzheimer's disease, and arthritis. Researchers at King's College in London have found that tea contains some health-giving stuff that could help with all of this. The good chemicals in tea, called antioxidants, can zap the free radicals, and drinking a few cups every day can strengthen bones and cut your chances of a heart attack. Your teeth can benefit too, because tea protects against plaque and decay, and it also contains fluoride.

So, if you aren't drinking one of the poisonous, poopy

eighteenth-century versions, tea is a wholesome pick-me-up. But there have been many "health drinks" through history that were actually really harmful. It's pretty unbelievable to us today, but there was a time when the addictive and dangerous drug cocaine was in common and legal use in a kind of energy drink!

In 1863, the French chemist Angelo Mariani invented "Vin Mariani," which was wine treated with coca leaves, the active ingredient of which is cocaine. In those days, the terrible effects of this drug weren't understood, and the drink became a huge success.

In fact, one of the wine's main marketing tricks was the nineteenth-century version of the influencer endorsement. Celebrities such as the army general and future president Ulysses S. Grant, the actress Sarah Bernhardt, the writer Jules Verne, and even the pope all spoke publicly about the drink's benefits. And as a man who wanted to fit as much useful work as possible into his life, the famous inventor Thomas Edison was known to drink Vin Mariani on a regular basis.

From the 1860s, cocaine could be found not just in drinks, but also in medicines everywhere, and it was advertised as a cure-all. The fictional detective Sherlock Holmes is described as using it on a regular basis. You could even buy cocaine cigarettes, which was a double whammy of wrong! Cocaine was especially loved by those who suffered from hay fever. In fact, the United States Hay Fever Association made the drug its official remedy in the 1880s.

But by the very early twentieth century, the authorities in the United States began to crack down on dangerous foods and drugs like cocaine. In 1906, the government founded what would later become known as the Food and Drug Administration (FDA), which is responsible for protecting public health by making sure products are safe to consume. Around this time, a version of Angelo Mariani's wine that contained no coca extract went on sale. But buyers continued getting their fix from another drink on the market: Coca-Cola. A "pinch of coca leaves" was included in John Stith Pemberton's original recipe for Coke, and the drink was advertised as a nerve tonic. But by 1929, all traces of the coca leaf were being left out of the popular drink—though we still wouldn't call Coke a "healthy" beverage today!

Throughout the ages, many of the things we eat and drink have been held up to us as medical miracles, or slammed as life-sucking poisons. But if the past has taught us anything, it's that putting all our faith in a single cure-all—whether it's cabbage, or Coca-Cola, or colon removal—can be a risky business. So, next time someone tries to sell you one simple remedy as the key to a healthy life, remind them that history's snake-oil salesmen have often had to eat humble pie!

A TASTE OF THEIR OWN MEDICINE . . .

Around the turn of the nineteenth century, an American nutritionist named Horace Fletcher made a lot of money promoting his weight-loss plan. This involved, quite simply, chewing your food . . . A LOT. Horace's thinking was that you should only chow down when you're really hungry, and then you could eat any food you like, as long as you ground it down and down between your teeth, until all of the liquid came out of it. Then you should swallow the liquid, and spit the rest out.

His program became really popular and was known as "Fletcherism." Another word for chewing is "masticating," and Horace became famous in the press as the "Great Masticator."

The problem was that spitting everything else out meant there was no fiber—the stuff you can't digest—in your diet, and you would become hopelessly constipated. Which is exactly what happened to Horace. His bowels became so backed up with poop that they were pushing up against his lungs, and making him short of breath. He also fasted a lot, and when he did take a meal, he would eat only a small number of foods that weren't giving him the nutrients he needed. So, he destroyed his own health, and died relatively young.

Although any diet that tells you not to swallow your food is dangerous and will leave you lacking in vital nutrients, scientists today do agree with Horace about the benefits of chewing thoroughly. It takes your gut quite a long time to tell your brain that you feel full when you're eating. The faster you gobble your lunch, the more of it you will want to have. Taking in food slowly and chewing it well does help people regulate their food intake.

LAST GASPS

Breathtaking triumphs and disasters to do with lungs

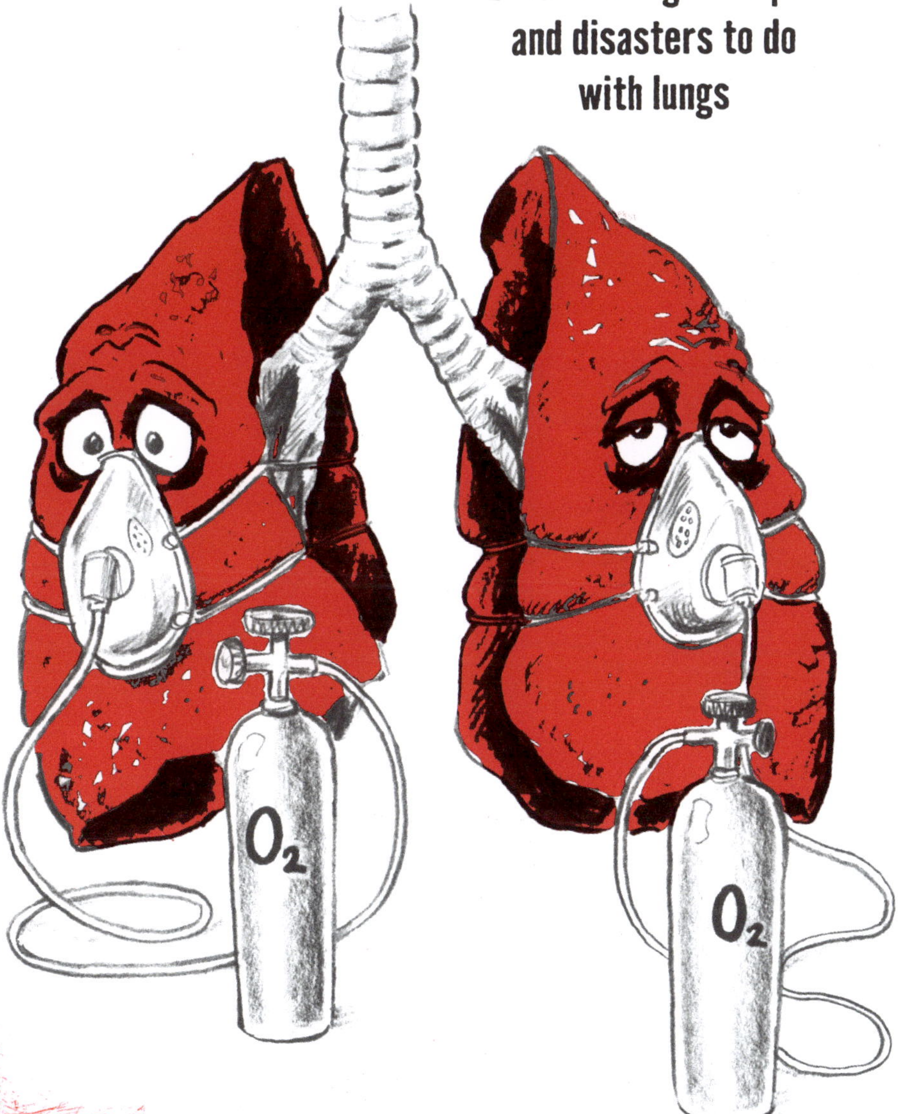

IT WAS A COLD Scottish morning in December of 1732 when James Blair descended into the depths of the local mine, along with several other coal workers. Weeks before, there had been a fire in the mine, forcing the authorities to seal it off in order to smother the flames. When it was reopened, James was among the first to enter its access shaft.

As the miners reached the bottom, however, they began to choke on thick smoke trapped in the deepest chambers. The men scurried back up the ladder, gasping for air. Only when they reached the top did they realize that poor James was still two hundred feet underground.

William Tossach, the town's doctor, arrived at the scene just as rescuers pulled James from the shaft. William found that the miner wasn't breathing and he couldn't feel a pulse. The doctor later described what he did next: "I applied my Mouth close to his, and blowed my Breath as strong as I could, but having neglected to stop his Nostrils, all the Air came out at them."

After this bad start, William realized that pinching the nostrils together would stop the immediate escape of air, and so he tried again. James soon regained consciousness and was able to return to work a week later. Although he didn't invent the technique, William's description is one of the earliest recorded cases of a person being successfully revived by mouth-to-mouth resuscitation.

Mouth-to-mouth resuscitation was a really valuable medical innovation, but also an incredibly simple one! It involves no fancy equipment or miraculous medicine. But like so many medical triumphs, it didn't change the world overnight. After all, William's success didn't immediately make mouth-to-mouth resuscitation standard practice because not enough people read about the success of a small-town doctor to lead to its widespread use. But

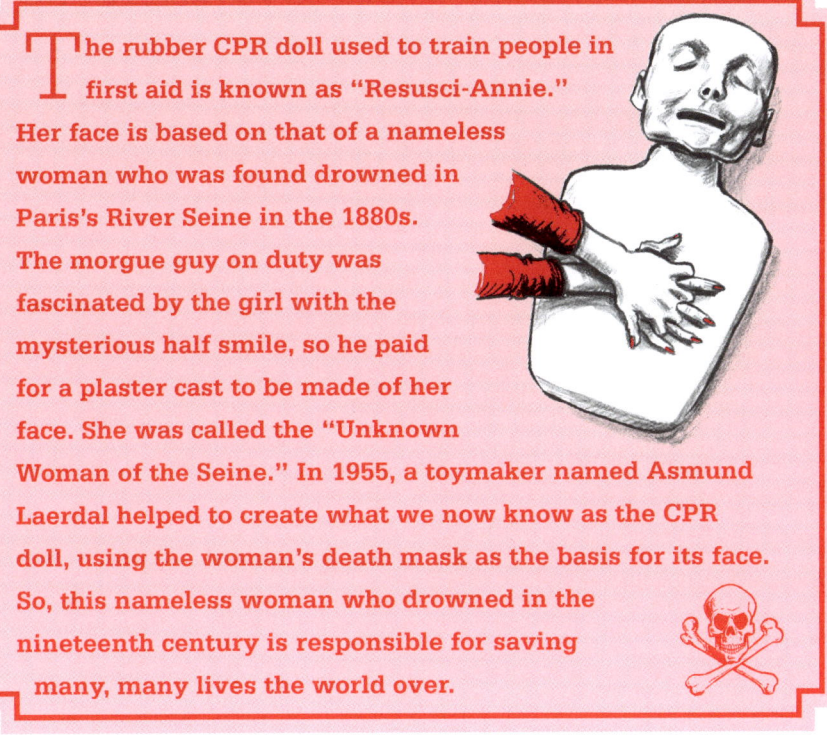

The rubber CPR doll used to train people in first aid is known as "Resusci-Annie." Her face is based on that of a nameless woman who was found drowned in Paris's River Seine in the 1880s. The morgue guy on duty was fascinated by the girl with the mysterious half smile, so he paid for a plaster cast to be made of her face. She was called the "Unknown Woman of the Seine." In 1955, a toymaker named Asmund Laerdal helped to create what we now know as the CPR doll, using the woman's death mask as the basis for its face. So, this nameless woman who drowned in the nineteenth century is responsible for saving many, many lives the world over.

perhaps the most interesting thing about this story is that it backs up the old saying "necessity is the mother of invention." This is a fancy-pants way of saying that when the need for a solution becomes urgent enough, people will do what it takes to find one.

Long before William Trossach breathed life back into James Blair, our old friend, the brilliant Flemish doctor and anatomist Andreas Vesalius made an opening in a dog's throat and inserted a reed tube. Through this tube, he blew air into the dog's lungs. This simple technique, which doctors now call a "tracheotomy," is still used today to help people with blocked airways breathe.

Andreas's experiment showed the power of mechanical ventilation, which is helping someone to breathe by outside means, though it would not become a standard medical procedure for centuries to come. This was partly due to the fact that doctors didn't yet fully understand the purpose of breathing, or "respiration"—which was a bit of a fail itself! In fact, figuring out what our lungs are all about, and how to help them when disease strikes, took a seriously long while.

For over a thousand years, doctors had to rely on just their ears to hear the inner sounds of the human body. This was one of the only ways to diagnose stuff like chest infections in patients. In 350 BCE, Hippocrates—the ancient Greek "Father of Medicine"—suggested gently shaking the patient by the shoulders, while putting your ear against their chest in order to hear the rattling of pus in the lungs.

This went unchanged for more than *two thousand years*! Like

our other old friend Galen, Hippocrates was one of those ancient-world guys hardly anyone was brave enough to question for far too long. But in 1816, things finally changed. A French doctor named René Laënnec was caring for a very sick girl. René tapped on her upper body with his fingers—a technique called percussion—to try to hear if fluid had gathered around her heart and lungs.

Unfortunately, this didn't work. He then considered pressing his ear to her chest, as Hippocrates advised so long ago, but he rejected this idea as inappropriate due to the girl's young age. Desperate to find a solution, René changed tactics. He rolled some sheets of paper into a tube, then touched one end of it to the area of the heart, and the other to his ear. He was very surprised and

RENÉ LAËNNEC

pleased to find that he could hear the patient's heartbeat much more clearly than he had ever been able to using just his ear.

René then made a wooden version of his tube. It was a simple hollow cylinder with only one earpiece. Eventually, he called this instrument a "stethoscope," from the Greek words meaning "I see" and "the chest."

Within a few years, René's invention could be found proudly displayed in the windows of medical shops around Paris. By the 1890s, the stethoscope would have its more familiar shape of two earpieces and a bell-shaped end. This medical instrument became super successful and incredibly popular with doctors. For the first time in history, you could listen really clearly to the internal workings of the body.

But René didn't have long to enjoy his success. He had spent many years of his life studying lung diseases before he was brought down by one himself, in 1826. He was suffering from a disease called tuberculosis (often shortened to TB). This was a global killer, claiming the lives of one in seven people. It's caused by a bacterium, and it has terrible effects on the lungs, leading to coughing, chills, fevers, and weight loss.

René asked his nephew to listen to his chest using his stethoscope. The nephew heard exactly the kind of sounds that René

In ancient Greece, doctors believed that air passed through the arteries, which we now know transport blood throughout the body. The origin of the word "artery" is from the Greek word *arteria*, meaning "windpipe." This misunderstanding arose from the fact that after a person dies, the arteries have no blood in them. And doctors in ancient Greece were only examining the inside of dead bodies.

had heard a thousand times in his dying patients. A few months later, René lost his battle with the disease he had worked so hard to explain and describe, dying at the young age of forty-five. It was thanks to his own invention that he had become aware of his unavoidable end. The stethoscope has become one of the most famous symbols of medicine, and it is still with us today. Like mouth-to-mouth resuscitation, it was a simple solution born out of necessity—and it only took two thousand years!

Unfortunately, being able to hear and identify tuberculosis didn't stop it from spreading wildly and killing a lot of people. The war with the disease raged for a long time. In 1890, the famous German scientist Robert Koch thought he'd created a substance that could protect people against the disease, and sometimes even cure it. He called his discovery Tuberculin (*really* imaginative naming there, Robert, well done). It was a mixture of stuff taken from the tuberculosis

ROBERT KOCH

bacterium itself, and Robert thought an injection of it could stop the germs from developing in the body.

Fantastic, right? Well, not really. Although the world got super excited about the idea of a cure, it turned out Tuberculin didn't work, and it actually made a lot of people sick. Robert's reputation took a big hit as a result. But proving that medicine's mistakes can sometimes be unexpectedly useful, it was later found that Tuberculin was a great tool for *testing* people for tuberculosis.

The test involves injecting a small amount of Tuberculin under the skin and waiting for any signs like reddening, swelling, or blistering. A reaction shows that the body's immune system has been dealing with tuberculosis all along, proving that the patient already has the disease. This test is still the most common way to diagnose tuberculosis today. Like the stethoscope, it's a solution invented ages ago that's still with us. Not a bad turnaround for a mistake from more than 130 years ago!

A hundred years before Tuberculin was invented, a guy named Joseph Priestley tried his hand at treating TB. You may remember that he was a colleague of Humphry Davy, the laughing gas fan. Joseph had caught TB himself when he was a teenager, and this inspired him to study the disease in the hopes of treating it. Around this time, scientists were just beginning to understand that "air" was made up of different gases. Joseph worked at an institute that was set up to investigate how these newly discovered gases might help treat diseases of the lungs.

Unfortunately, Joseph's work on TB never panned out. But in 1774, he contributed hugely to our understanding of the lungs by discovering oxygen. At that same time, two other scientists named

Carl Wilhelm Scheele and Antoine Lavoisier identified the gas, too. It was in large part thanks to Antoine that the role of oxygen in breathing was figured out. But this success led to a setback. There was a temporary pause in the use of mouth-to-mouth resuscitation, since doctors worried that exhaled air might lack the vital agent, oxygen. (In reality, exhaled air contains quite a lot of oxygen, and at least enough for resuscitation.)

William Henry Harrison, the ninth president of the USA, died in 1841, only thirty-two days after his inaugural speech. He spoke for over two hours without his hat, coat, or gloves on a bitterly cold day. He grew sick shortly afterward. This turned into pneumonia—an infection that causes the lungs to fill with fluid or pus. Doctors tried everything from bloodletting to a Native American remedy involving a live snake. But it was no use. William died, after the shortest period in office of any US president. People blamed his illness on "a chill," which we now know is totally bogus because cold weather can't give you an infection.

Through much of the eighteenth and nineteenth centuries, doctors didn't understand that when a person passed out, it was related to a lack of oxygen in their lungs. Instead, they believed that it was due to a lack of stimulation in the body. In the same year that oxygen was discovered, the Society for the Recovery of Persons Apparently Drowned was founded in England. A huge number of people were drowning because hardly anyone was taught to swim in childhood. In 1773 alone, 123 people drowned in London. To encourage resuscitation attempts, the society offered cash prizes to those who could prove they had successfully revived a victim of drowning.

As a result, the need to solve the problem led to some truly weird experiments, including rolling drowned people over barrels, throwing them onto a trotting horse, hanging them upside down, cooling them on ice, and even giving them a good whipping. The strangest one of all involved tobacco smoke, which some people believed fought cold and drowsiness, and had life-giving powers. At various points along London's River Thames, the society placed resuscitator kits containing bellows that could be used to blow tobacco smoke into drowned people's lungs, stomachs, or even up their butts! After all of that nonsense, you've gotta think people would be happier to stay drowned.

Whether it was René Laennec's brilliant stethoscope, or the very not-brilliant bellows up the butthole, doctors were always looking for machines that could help treat the inside of the body. A really deadly disease forced them to come up with something ground-breaking in the first half of the twentieth century.

At that time, a virus called polio was the leading cause of death in children and young adults. In the worst cases, it causes a kind of paralysis, which can make breathing impossible. Few diseases were more dreaded by parents. An outbreak in Brooklyn in 1916 led to the widespread closure of movie theaters, parks, and swimming pools. The names and addresses of the infected were published daily in newspapers in an attempt to prevent the illness from spreading. Warning notices were nailed to their doors, and entire families were forced to remain locked away from the wider population.

By the 1920s, the situation had become critical. One day Philip Drinker—a hygienist from the Harvard School of Public Health—visited a hospital to fix a problem with the air-conditioning. He was deeply upset by the sight of children with polio struggling to breathe. And so Philip set out to do something about it.

Remember Andreas Vesalius, who blew air into a dog's throat through a reed in the sixteenth century? That was really basic mechanical ventilation: helping a person (or a dog) breathe when they can't do so on their own. But it wasn't until the nineteenth century that we started creating machines that could take on this job.

In 1832, a Scottish doctor named John Dalziel invented the "tank respirator," which could push air in and out of the lungs. The patient sat upright in a sealed box with only their head and neck poking out. A device called a piston, which looked a bit like a bicycle pump, sucked air out of the box. This forced patients

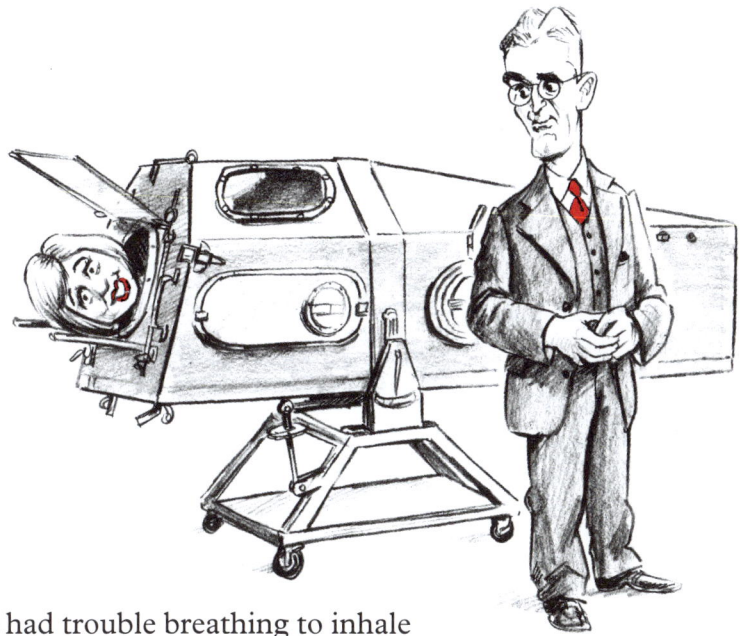

who had trouble breathing to inhale
through the mouth and nose. John's machine was a success, and
soon others were trying to create their own designs that could
keep people alive. But each had flaws to overcome. One design
needed the sick patients to pump air in and out of the machine
themselves!

Nearly one hundred years later, a breakthrough finally came
thanks in part to technological advances that weren't available to
earlier doctors. That's where Philip Drinker comes back into the
story. With the help of his colleague Louis Agassiz Shaw, Philip
invented a contraption called an "iron lung." Powered by an electric motor, the machine acted like a vacuum—creating and releas-
ing pressure around the body to simulate breathing while the
patient lay inside it with only their head exposed—sort of like the
tank respirator, but a lot more efficient. (The name "iron lung" is
not totally accurate because the machine doesn't mimic the lungs,

but rather, it mimics the muscles that fill and empty the lungs!) Drinker's invention was first used at Boston Children's Hospital in 1928 to treat an eight-year-old girl.

So, that must be the happy ending of this great success story, right? Well, no. As effective as the iron lung was, the machine was bulky and expensive. While some hospitals had plenty of iron lungs, others had too few. And this was a serious problem when there were big outbreaks of polio.

In 1952, over 2,700 patients in Copenhagen were rushed to the hospital with polio. Ironically, it had started to spread after the city had hosted an international medical conference on the virus. Many of the doctors who had come to learn more about polio were unknowingly bringing it with them into the population!

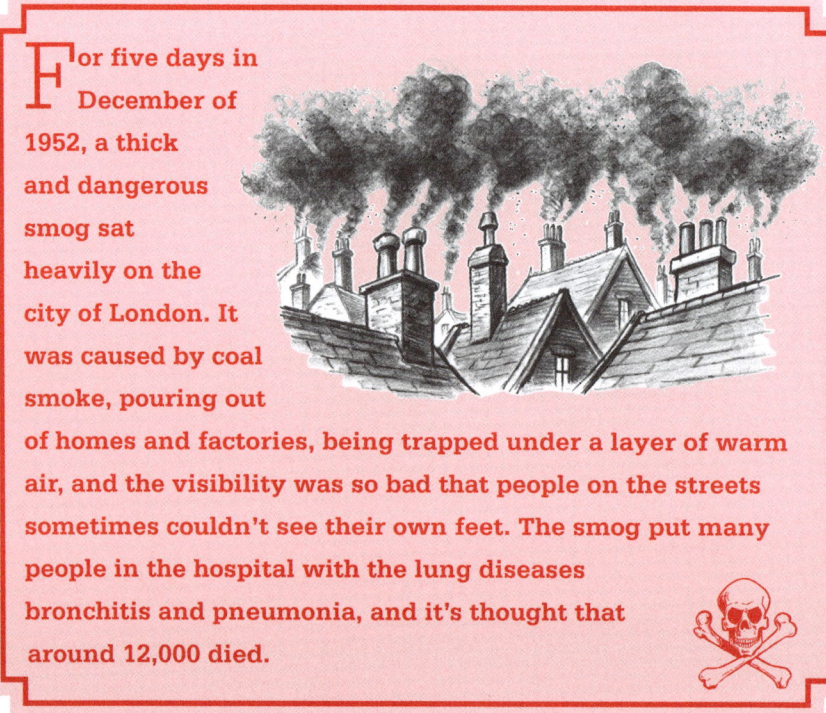

For five days in December of 1952, a thick and dangerous smog sat heavily on the city of London. It was caused by coal smoke, pouring out of homes and factories, being trapped under a layer of warm air, and the visibility was so bad that people on the streets sometimes couldn't see their own feet. The smog put many people in the hospital with the lung diseases bronchitis and pneumonia, and it's thought that around 12,000 died.

Soon, the hospital staff was overwhelmed by the number of sick patients coming onto the wards. It was the largest-ever polio epidemic in Europe to date.

Doctors placed the sickest patients in iron lungs, but they didn't have nearly enough of the machines. And there was another problem. Breathing requires that we not just take oxygen *into* our lungs through inhaling, but that we also *get rid of* dangerous carbon dioxide through exhaling. The iron lung didn't allow patients to exhale fully, and some were dying as a result of the buildup of the harmful gas in their systems.

The hospital turned to a doctor named Bjørn Ibsen for help. Building on the research of others, he developed a system to blow air directly into people's lungs—much like Andreas Vesalius did with the dog centuries earlier. Bjørn picked a twelve-year-old girl named Vivi, who was extremely sick and unlikely to live much longer. He sliced into her throat, inserted a tube, and attached a rubber bag filled with an oxygen supply. With each squeeze of the bag, air filled her lungs.

BJØRN IBSEN

Unfortunately, Vivi began bucking and spasming. So, Bjørn gave her a drug to calm her down. Before long, Vivi had stopped moving. The other doctors who had come to see Bjørn's efforts assumed the child would die, and left. But Bjørn wouldn't give up. He continued pumping the bag over and over again, each time forcing air into Vivi's lungs. Soon, color returned to her cheeks. Vivi would live if Bjørn could just keep squeezing the bag. When the other doctors returned to the room, they were amazed at what they saw.

Over the next eight days, the hospital organized bag ventilation for every patient who needed it. It was a huge challenge. At times, as many as seventy patients needed around-the-clock ventilation, which required 250 ten-liter gas cylinders each day. The hospital recruited 1,500 medical and dental students, who took turns ventilating the patients. Miraculously, none of the volunteers caught polio during this time.

Slowly, patients were weaned off ventilation as their muscle strength improved. There were some, however, who were still unable to breathe on their own, even a year later. Some of these patients never regained the function and would need help from machines like the iron lung for the rest of their lives.

Today, Bjørn Ibsen is known as the founder of intensive-care medicine, which provides around-the-clock observation and treatment to dangerously ill patients. His solution to the polio outbreak in Denmark was born out of dire need, and it also turned out to be a rather simple solution in the end!

In 1963—a year before he transplanted a chimpanzee's heart into a patient—Dr. James Hardy was thinking about lungs. He had been transplanting them into animals in his laboratory for some time, and he was ready to try it on a human.

On April 15, a potential candidate for a lung transplant named John Russell was brought into the University of Mississippi Medical Center, where James worked. John was very sick. He would lie awake at night coughing up blood until he was blue in the face. He felt like he could never catch his breath.

James ran a bunch of tests and discovered that John had cancer in his left lung, which made him an ideal candidate for a new lung. There was just one hitch: John was a murderer who was serving a life sentence in prison. (By the way, there was no discussion about what would happen if the doc helped him survive, or whether his prison sentence would be reduced.)

James explained to John the risks of undergoing an operation that had never been attempted before. These included organ rejection, which happens when the body attacks the new organ because it thinks it's a foreign object. Organ rejection can lead to death. But despite the dangers, John agreed to go ahead with the surgery.

It was nearly two months before a donor arrived. A patient had suffered a heart attack and could not be resuscitated. And so—as it often turns out in medicine—one person's bad luck becomes another's lucky break. James received permission from the dead person's family to remove one of the lungs and try to give it a new home inside John.

On June 11, James and his team opened up John's chest to begin the transplant. That's when they saw that his cancer had spread. If the lung transplant was successful, it would not save his life. But James and his team hoped it might help John breathe more easily, so they went ahead with the operation.

Initially, the surgery was a success, and the new lung did help to improve John's breathing. James used a cocktail of drugs and radiation to ensure that John's body accepted its new lung. But eighteen days later, the patient died from kidney failure, likely brought on by the very treatment he was undergoing to prevent organ rejection. Doctors still could not overcome this major medical hurdle.

Over the next seven years, twenty-three further human lung transplantations were performed by twenty different surgeons. All but one patient died within one month of the operation. The single survivor only lived for ten months. And yet doctors kept going, convinced that they would one day be successful. And they were right to stick with it, because later advances in immunology would crack the problem of organ rejection. This, coupled with other breakthroughs like blood typing, finally made transplant surgery possible.

Today, over 40,000 organ transplant surgeries are performed each year in the USA alone, giving hope to countless people for a new chance of life. And the seeds of that success had been sown in the field of failure.

A TASTE OF THEIR OWN MEDICINE . . .

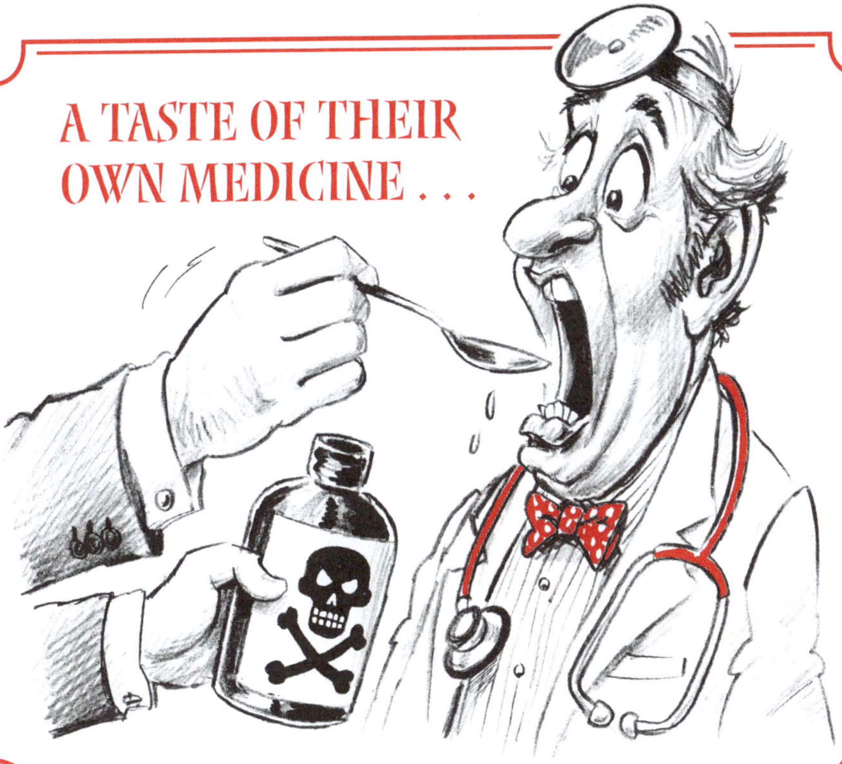

In 1933, Evarts A. Graham became the first surgeon ever to remove a lung as a treatment for cancer.

Evarts's patient, who was also a doctor, had been a lifetime smoker. When he was diagnosed, he put off having the operation and even bought himself a grave plot in a cemetery. But he didn't take account of how brilliant a surgeon Evarts was. At last, he gave in.

The procedure only took an hour and forty-five minutes, and it was so successful it became a very big deal among doctors around the world, giving a real boost to the development of modern lung cancer treatment. Evarts stayed friends with his patient, and he used to invite him to meetings with other surgeons. In spite of continuing to smoke, he went on to survive for thirty years!

Evarts, however, wasn't as lucky as his patient. He died in 1957, long before the man he had saved. And the cause of Evart's death? Lung cancer. The surgeon had given up a lifetime of smoking after his research suggested a link between the habit and lung disease. But it was too late.

AFTERWORD

NEW YORK CITY'S CONEY Island—with its fairground rides, carnival sideshows, and hot dog vendors—might seem like an unusual place to spark a medical revolution. But by now, we hope you will have figured out that success can grow out of the weirdest and most unpromising beginnings.

If you could travel back in time and visit the famous amusement park at the start of the twentieth century, you wouldn't have just come across a Ferris wheel and roller coasters. You would also have seen a newfangled machine called an incubator. It had been brought to the park by a forward-thinking guy who had made it his life's mission to save the lives of infants born too early. He thought

Coney Island was the perfect place to advertise this equipment to the world . . . using real babies! Why did he need to advertise this innovation at all? Because the medical world thought incubators were a total waste of time.

Incubators are machines that keep delicate premature babies warm and protect them from the outside environment. This is important because their bodies aren't developed enough to do this for themselves. A French doctor named Stéphane Tarnier had adapted incubators for human infants after he first saw them being used to raise baby birds in a zoo. But doctors weren't convinced of their usefulness. This was partly because they thought incubators weren't scientific, but mostly because they thought that trying to save the lives of sickly premature babies was pointless since most died shortly after birth.

Even when another French doctor named Pierre Budin carried out encouraging scientific research into incubators, most hospitals didn't want to know. So, Pierre took his case to the people, putting some working models on display at the world's fair in Berlin, Germany, in 1896. He saved the lives of six babies in the process, and the public was amazed. So, too, was a man named Martin Couney. His own daughter had been born prematurely and had survived against the odds, but he knew there were many babies who were not so lucky. Inspired by what he had witnessed at the world's fair, Martin decided to give this new wonder-tech as big a platform as he could think of. And so he traveled to the USA to set up two incubator displays at Coney Island in 1903.

The crowds flocked and paid an entrance fee to see a row of babies sleeping and growing stronger in the warmth of their life-saving machines. Martin didn't charge the parents for this service, and the ticket proceeds were put toward the care of the infants. By his calculations, his truly astonishing fairground sideshow saved the lives of around 6,500 children over forty years. By 1943, when he finally closed the exhibit, doctors had accepted that they had been wrong about incubators, and soon these miracle machines were appearing in hospitals all over the world. Today, they are an essential tool for those trying to save the lives of the one in ten babies who are born prematurely.

As we've shown throughout this book, the history of medicine is a long tale of trying and failing, trying again, failing again, and failing better. Through centuries of missteps, mistakes, and misunderstandings, doctors have come to a better understanding of the human body and the best ways to treat it. Sometimes this was down to one determined individual pursuing what seemed for a while like a crazy idea, in the face of nothing but naysayers. Sometimes it was down to whole groups of people learning from each other's setbacks over a long, long stretch of time.

And sure, some disasters were all downside. But many medical mistakes led unexpectedly to real breakthroughs that still benefit us in the present—like Robert Koch's Tuberculin, Wilson Greatbatch's pacemakers, and James Hanger's prosthetic limbs. A lot of history's foul-ups have also led to the creation of agencies like the Food and Drug Administration, and to a host of other safeguards that help protect the public from harm.

Nobody likes to fail. But what looks like a dead end is sometimes

just a change of direction in disguise. When all is said and done, the moral of our story is that failure should be our teacher, not our undertaker.

ACKNOWLEDGMENTS

IN A BOOK ABOUT failure and success, it's fitting that we pay tribute to those without whom our attempts to conduct readers on an energetic romp through some truly obscure corners of history would have ended in blisters, twisted ankles, and mutual recrimination.

At Bloomsbury, we'd like to thank our dedicated editor, Megan Abbate, and the talented John Candell, whose fantastic design skills have put so much pep in this book's step. Thanks too to our agent, Robert Guinsler. And a special mention goes to Caroline Overy, whose close reading of the first draft has been invaluable.

As ever, we would like to offer our sincere gratitude to our family, and to our two fat cats, Oscar and Bobo, whose interest in our work extends only as far as whether it will help maintain the lifestyle to which they are accustomed.

SELECTED SOURCES

Lindsey has a doctorate in the history of science and medicine, and has studied the subject all her adult life. Here is a select number of sources that she has found useful over the years, and that helped in the making of this book. Adrian likes the ones with pictures in them.

Introduction

Fitzharris, Lindsey. *The Butchering Art: Joseph Lister's Quest to Transform the Grisly World of Victorian Medicine*. New York: Scientific American / Farrar, Straus and Giroux, 2017.

Hollingham, Richard. *Blood and Guts: A History of Surgery*. London: BBC Books, 2008.

Porter, Roy. *Blood and Guts: A Short History of Medicine*. New York: W. W. Norton & Company, 2003.

Porter, Roy. *Disease, Medicine and Society in England, 1550–1860*. 2nd ed. Cambridge: Cambridge University Press, 1995.

Porter, Roy. *The Greatest Benefit to Mankind: A Medical History of Humanity*. New York: W.W. Norton & Company, 1998.

Youngson, A. J. *The Scientific Revolution in Victorian Medicine*. London: Croom Helm, 1979.

Head-Shakers

Andress, David. *The Terror. Civil War in the French Revolution*. London: Abacus, 2006.

Craddock, Paul. *Spare Parts. A Surprising History of Transplants*. London: Penguin, 2021.

Deniker, J. "J. V. Laborde (1830–1903)." *Nature* 68 (June 1903): 106.

Faria, Miguel A. "Neolithic Trepanation Decoded—A Unifying Hypothesis: Has the Mystery as to Why Primitive Surgeons Performed Cranial Surgery Been Solved?" *Surgical Neurology International* 6 (May 2016): 72.

Gerabek, W. E. "The Tooth-Worm: Historical Aspects of a Popular Belief." *Clinical Oral Investigations* 3, no. 1 (March 1999): 1–6.

Kershaw, Alister. *A History of the Guillotine*. London: John Calder, 1958.

Krishnan, Prasad, and Shubhrajit Nag. "Historical Vignette: Andreas Vesalius and Head Injuries in Royalty." *Asian Journal of Neurosurgery* 16, no. 3 (September 2021): 663–664.

Larson, Frances. *Severed: A History of Heads Lost and Heads Found*. London: Granta Books, 2015.

Moore, Wendy. *The Knife Man: Blood, Body-Snatching and the Birth of Modern Surgery*. London: Bantam, 2006.

Morris, Thomas. *The Mystery of Exploding Teeth and Other Curiosities from the History of Medicine*. London: Dutton, 2018.

Porter, Dorothy, and Roy Porter. *Patient's Progress: Doctors and Doctoring in Eighteenth-Century England*. Cambridge: Polity Press, 1989.

Quigley, Christine. *The Corpse: A History*. Jefferson, North Carolina: McFarland & Company, Inc., Publishers, 1996.

Roach, Mary. *Stiff: The Curious Lives of Human Cadavers*. New York: W. W. Norton & Company, 2003.

Rosner, Lisa. *The Anatomy Murders: Being the True and Spectacular History of Edinburgh's Notorious Burke and Hare and of the Man of Science Who Abetted Them in the Commission of Their Most Heinous Crimes*. Philadelphia: University of Pennsylvania Press, 2011.

Schama, Simon. *Citizens: A Chronicle of the French Revolution*. London: Penguin, 2004.

Soubiran, André. *The Good Doctor Guillotin and His Strange Device*. Translated by Malcolm MacCraw. London: Souvenir Press, 1964.

Sugg, Richard. *Mummies, Cannibals, and Vampires: The History of Corpse Medicine from the Renaissance to the Victorians*. London: Routledge, 2011.

Zubairi, Ramsha. "The Shocking Medical History of Electric Fish: How a Piscine Biomedical Tradition Stretching from Ancient Egypt to Colonial Guyana Helped Create the First Batteries." *Long Now,* April 2023, online at https://longnow.org/ideas/the-shocking-medical-history-of-electric-fish/ (accessed November 5, 2024).

Racking Your Brains

Akkermans, Rebecca. "David Ferrier." *The Lancet Neurology* 15, no. 7 (June 2016): 666.

Caplan, Eric Michael. "Trains, Brains, and Sprains: Railway Spine and the Origins of Psychoneuroses." *Bulletin of the History of Medicine* 69, no. 3 (1995): 387–419.

Damasio, Antonio R. *Descartes' Error: Emotion, Reason, and the Human Brain.* New York: Avon, 1994.

Fishman, Ronald S. "Ferrier's Mistake Revisited, or When It Comes to the Brain, Nothing Is Simple." *Archives of Neurology* 52, no. 7 (1995): 725–730.

Fleischman, John. *Phineas Gage: A Gruesome but True Story about Brain Science*. Boston: Houghton Mifflin, 2002.

Gasquoine, Philip Gerard. "Railway Spine: The Advent of Compensation for Concussive Symptoms." *Journal of the History of the Neurosciences* 29, no. 2 (2020): 234–245.

Kean, Sam. *The Icepick Surgeon: Murder, Fraud, Sabotage, Piracy, and Other Dastardly Deeds Perpetrated in the Name of Science*. Boston: Little Brown and Company, 2021.

Keller, Thomas, and Thomas Chappell. "The Rise and Fall of Erichsen's Disease (Railroad Spine)." *Spine* 21, no. 13 (July 1996): 1597–1601.

Lazar J. Wayne. "David Ferrier: Brain Drawings and Brain Maps." *Progress in Brain Research* 203 (2013): 95–113.

Mitchell, Kevin J. *Innate: How the Wiring of Our Brains Shapes Who We Are.* Princeton: Princeton University Press, 2020.

Porter, Roy. *Blood and Guts: A Short History of Medicine.* New York: W. W. Norton & Company, 2003.

Schillace, Brandy. *Mr. Humble and Dr. Butcher: A Monkey's Head, the Pope's Neuroscientist, and the Quest to Transplant the Soul.* New York: Simon & Schuster, 2021.

Life and Limb

Adams, Aileen K. "Tarnished Idol: William Thomas Green Morton and the Introduction of Surgical Anesthesia." *Journal of the Royal Society of Medicine* 95, no. 5 (2002): 266–267.

Chaturvedi, Ravindra, and R. L. Gogna. "Ether Day: An Intriguing History." *Medical Journal Armed Forces India* 67, no. 4 (2011): 306–308.

Demaitre, Luke. *Medieval Medicine: The Art of Healing, from Head to Toe.* West Port, Connecticut, and London: Praeger, 2013.

Ellis, Harold. *A History of Surgery.* London: Greenwich Medical Media, 2001.

Hartnell, Jack. *Medieval Bodies: Life, Death and Art in the Middle Ages.* London: Wellcome Collection, 2018.

Hedrick, Elizabeth. "Romancing the Salve: Sir Kenelm Digby and the Powder of Sympathy." *British Journal for the History of Science* 41, no. 2 (2008): 161–185.

Hollingham, Richard. *Blood and Guts: A History of Surgery.* London: BBC Books, 2008.

Ingraham, Chris. *Enabling the Human Spirit: The J. E. Hanger Story.* Pittsburgh: Word Association Publishers, 2003.

Porter, Roy. *The Greatest Benefit to Mankind: A Medical History of Humanity.* New York: W. W. Norton & Company, 1998.

Robinson, Victor. *Victory over Pain: A History of Anesthesia.* London: Sigma Books, 1947.

Snow, Stephanie J. *Blessed Days of Anaesthesia: How Anaesthetics Changed the World*. Oxford: Oxford University Press, 2008.

Sugg, Richard. *Mummies, Cannibals, and Vampires: The History of Corpse Medicine from the Renaissance to the Victorians*. London: Routledge, 2011.

Sykes, Keith, and John Bunker. *Anaesthesia and the Practice of Medicine: Historical Perspectives*. Boca Raton, Florida: CRC Press, 2007.

Washington University in St. Louis. "Older Neanderthal Survived with a Little Help from His Friends." *ScienceDaily*, October 23, 2017, online at www.sciencedaily.com/releases/2017/10/171023181552.htm (accessed November 4, 2024).

Winter, Alison. *Mesmerized: Powers of the Mind in Victorian Britain*. Chicago: University of Chicago Press, 1998.

Bleeding Hearts

Brink, Johan G., and Joannis Hassoulas. "The First Human Heart Transplant and Further Advances in Cardiac Transplantation at Groote Schuur Hospital and the University of Cape Town." *Cardiovascular Journal of Africa* 20, no. 1 (2009): 31–35.

Chaikhouni, Amer. "The Magnificent Century of Cardiothoracic Surgery." *Heart Views: The Official Journal of the Gulf Heart Association* 11, no. 1 (2010): 31–37.

Cobb, W. Montague. "Dr. Daniel Hale Williams." *Journal of the National Medical Association* 45, no. 5 (1953): 379–385.

Craddock, Paul. *Spare Parts: A Surprising History of Transplants*. London: Penguin, 2021.

Ellis, Richard H., and Aileen K. Adams. "Henry Souttar and Surgery of the Mitral Valve. Part I: The Surgeon and His Patient." *Journal of Medical Biography* 5, no. 1 (1997): 8–13.

Figueredo, Vincent M. *The Curious History of the Heart: A Cultural and Scientific Journey*. New York: Columbia University Press, 2023.

Fitzharris, Lindsey. "A Brief History of Ventilation." Wellcome Collection,

July 2, 2020, online at https://wellcomecollection.org/stories/a-brief -history-of-ventilation (accessed November 5, 2024).

Forrester, James S. *The Heart Healers: The Misfits, Mavericks, and Rebels Who Created the Greatest Medical Breakthrough of Our Lives*. New York: St. Martin's Press, 2015.

Furman, Seymour. "Early History of Cardiac Pacing and Defibrillation." *Indian Pacing and Electrophysiology Journal* 2, no.1 (2002): 2–3.

Jauhar, Sandeep. *Heart: A History*. London: Oneworld Publications, 2018.

Owen, James. "Egyptian Princess Mummy Had Oldest Known Heart Disease." *National Geographic,* April 15, 2011, online at https://www .nationalgeographic.com/science/article/110415-ancient-egypt -mummies-princess-heart-disease-health-science (accessed November 5, 2024).

Parent, André. "Giovanni Aldini: From Animal Electricity to Human Brain Stimulation." *Canadian Journal of Neurological Sciences* 31 (2004): 576–584.

Stolf, Noedir A. G. "History of Heart Transplantation: A Hard and Glorious Journey." *Brazilian Journal of Cardiovascular Surgery* 32, no. 5 (2017): 423–427.

Weisse, Allen B. "Cardiac Surgery: A Century of Progress." *Texas Heart Institute Journal* 38, no. 5 (2011): 486–490.

Weisse, Allen B. "The Surgical Treatment of Mitral Stenosis: The First Heart Operation." *American Journal of Cardiology* 103, no. 1 (2009): 143–147.

Bad Blood

Fitzharris, Lindsey. "Bloodletting: Return of a Radical Remedy." *New Scientist,* November 14, 2012, online at https://www.newscientist.com /article/mg21628912-200-bloodletting-return-of-a-radical-remedy/ (accessed November 5, 2024).

Fitzharris, Lindsey. *The Facemaker: A Visionary Surgeon's Battle to Mend the Disfigured Soldiers of World War I*. New York: Farrar, Straus and Giroux, 2022.

George, Rose. *Nine Pints: A Journey Through the Mysterious, Miraculous World of Blood*. London: Portobello Books, 2018.

Keynes, Geoffrey. *Blood Transfusions*. Oxford: Oxford Medical Publications, 1922.

Pelling, Margaret. *Cholera, Fever, and English Medicine, 1825–1865*. Oxford: Oxford University Press, 1978.

Porter, Roy. *Blood and Guts: A Short History of Medicine*. New York: W. W. Norton & Company, 2003.

Sugg, Richard. *Mummies, Cannibals, and Vampires: The History of Corpse Medicine from the Renaissance to the Victorians*. London: Routledge, 2011.

Tucker, Holly. *Blood Work: A Tale of Medicine and Murder in the Scientific Revolution*. New York: W. W. Norton & Company, 2011.

Wain, S. L. "The Controversy of Unmodified versus Citrated Blood Transfusion in the Early 20th Century." *Historical Review* 24, no. 5 (1984): 404–407.

Worboys, Michael. *Spreading Germs: Disease Theories and Medical Practice in Britain, 1865–1900*. Cambridge: Cambridge University Press, 2000.

Zimmer, Carl. "Why Do We Have Blood Types?" BBC, July 14, 2014, online at https://www.bbc.com/future/article/20140715-why-do-we-have-blood -types (accessed November 5, 2024).

No Guts, No Glory

Bryson, Bill. *The Body: A Guide for Occupants*. New York: Doubleday, 2019.

Burki, Talha Khan. "William Arbuthnot Lane: Kink Catastrophe." *The Lancet Gastroenterology & Hepatology* 3, no. 10 (October 2018): 670.

Christen, A. G. "Horace Fletcher (1849–1919): 'The Great Masticator.'" *Journal of the History of Dentistry* 45, no. 3 (November 1997): 95–100.

Fee, Elizabeth, and Theodore M. Brown. "John Harvey Kellogg, MD: Health Reformer and Antismoking Crusader." *American Journal of Public Health* 92, no. 6 (2002): 935.

Fitzharris, Lindsey. *The Facemaker: A Visionary Surgeon's Battle to Mend the Disfigured Soldiers of World War I.* New York: Farrar, Straus and Giroux, 2022.

Foxcroft, Louise. *Calories and Corsets. A History of Dieting over 2,000 Years.* London: Profile Books, 2012.

Gale, Arthur. "Dr. William Beaumont: Founding Father of Gastroenterology." *Missouri Medicine* 118, no. 6 (2021): 518–519.

Kang, Lydia, and Nate Pedersen. *Quackery: A Brief History of the Worst Ways to Cure Everything.* New York: Workman Publishing Company, 2017.

Purnell, Carolyn. "Empirical Eating: 19th-Century Exotic Animal Consumption." *Psychology Today,* August 25, 2020, online at https://www.psychologytoday.com/gb/blog/making-sense/202008/empirical-eating-19th-century-exotic-animal-consumption (accessed October 31, 2024).

Raizman, Noah. "The Man with the Hole in His Side." *The Lancet* 379 (March 2012): 1188.

Smith, J. L. "Sir Arbuthnot Lane, Chronic Intestinal Stasis, and Autointoxication." *Annals of Internal Medicine* 96, no. 3 (March 1982): 365–369.

Standage, Tom. *An Edible History of Humanity.* New York: Bloomsbury USA, 2010.

Weisburger, John H. "Tea and Health: A Historical Perspective." *Cancer Letters* 114 (March 1997): 315–317.

White, Edward. "Me and My Monkey." *The Paris Review,* May 19, 2016, online at https://www.theparisreview.org/blog/2016/05/19/me-and-my-monkey/ (accessed April 3, 2024).

Whorton, James C. "'Physiologic Optimism': Horace Fletcher and Hygienic Ideology in Progressive America." *Bulletin of the History of Medicine* 55, no. 1 (1981): 59–87.

Last Gasps

Ackerknecht, Erwin H. *Medicine at the Paris Hospital, 1794–1848.* Baltimore: Johns Hopkins Press, 1967.

Barberis, I., N. L. Bragazzi, L. Galluzzo, and M. Martini. "The History of Tuberculosis: From the First Historical Records to the Isolation of Koch's Bacillus." *Journal of Preventive Medicine and Hygiene* 58, no. 1 (March 2017): E9–E12.

Barr, Marshall. "The Iron Lung—A Polio Patient's Story." *Journal of the Royal Society of Medicine* 103, no. 6 (2010): 256–259.

Brock, Thomas D. *Robert Koch: A Life in Medicine and Bacteriology*. Berlin: Springer, 1988.

Bynum, Helen. *Spitting Blood: The History of Tuberculosis*. Oxford: Oxford University Press, 2012.

Craddock, Paul. *Spare Parts. A Surprising History of Transplants*. London: Penguin, 2021.

DeBard, M. L. "The History of Cardiopulmonary Resuscitation." *Annals of Emergency Medicine* 9, no. 5 (May 1980): 273–275.

Fayssoil, Abdallah. "René Laennec (1781–1826) and the Invention of the Stethoscope." *American Journal of Cardiology* 104, no. 5 (June 2009): 743–744.

Fitzharris, Lindsey. "A Brief History of Ventilation." Wellcome Collection, July 2, 2020, online at https://wellcomecollection.org/stories/a-brief -history-of-ventilation (accessed November 5, 2024).

La Berge, Ann F. "Debate as Scientific Practice in Nineteenth-Century Paris: The Controversy over the Microscope," *Perspectives on Science* 12, no. 4 (2004): 425–427.

Lougheed, Kathryn. *Catching Breath: The Making and Unmaking of Tuberculosis*. London: Bloomsbury Sigma, 2017.

Meyer, J. A. "A Practical Mechanical Respirator, 1929: The 'Iron Lung.'" *Annals of Thoracic Surgery* 50, no. 3 (September 1990): 490–494.

Murray, John F., Dean E. Schraufnagel, and Philip C. Hopewell. "Treatment of Tuberculosis. A Historical Perspective." *Annals of the American Thoracic Society* 12, no. 12 (December 2015): 1749–1759.

Porter, Dorothy, and Roy Porter. *Patient's Progress: Doctors and Doctoring in Eighteenth-Century England*. Cambridge: Polity Press, 1989.

Reisner-Sénélar, Louise. "The Birth of Intensive Care Medicine: Björn Ibsen's Records." *Intensive Care Medicine* 37, no. 7 (July 2011): 1084–1086.

Richmond, Caroline. "Bjørn Ibsen." *British Medical Journal* 335, no. 7621 (2007): 674.

Roguin, Ariel. "Rene Theophile Hyacinthe Laënnec (1781–1826): The Man behind the Stethoscope." *Clinical Medicine & Research* 4, no. 3 (2006): 230–235.

Sloan, Marisa. "How a Parisian Death Mask Became the Face of CPR Dolls Everywhere." *Discover Magazine,* June 29, 2023, online at https://www.discovermagazine.com/the-sciences/how-a-parisian-death-mask-became-the-face-of-cprdolls-everywhere (accessed May 15, 2024).

Trubuhovich, Ronald V. "History of Mouth-to-Mouth Rescue Breathing. Part 2: The 18th Century." *Critical Care and Resuscitation* 8, no. 2 (June 2006): 157–171.

Youngson, A. J. *The Scientific Revolution in Victorian Medicine*. London: Croom Helm, 1979.

Afterword

Barry, Rebecca Rego. "Coney Island's Incubator Babies." *JSTOR Daily,* August 15, 2018, online at https://daily.jstor.org/coney-islands-incubator-babies/ (accessed November 4, 2024).

Prentice, Claire. "The Man Who Ran a Carnival Attraction That Saved Thousands of Premature Babies Wasn't a Doctor at All." *Smithsonian Magazine,* August 19, 2016, online at https://www.smithsonianmag.com/history/man-who-pretended-be-doctor-ran-worlds-fair-attraction-saved-lives-thousands-premature-babies-180960200/ (accessed November 5, 2024).

Yuko, Elizabeth. "The 'Child Hatchery' of Coney Island." *The Atlantic,* October 29, 2015, online at https://www.theatlantic.com/health/archive/2015/10/the-child-hatchery-of-coney-island/413080/ (accessed October 12, 2024).

FURTHER READING FOR FUTURE MEDICAL HISTORIANS

Fitzharris, Lindsey, and Adrian Teal. *Plague-Busters! Medicine's Battles with History's Deadliest Diseases*. New York: Bloomsbury Children's Books, 2023.

Fleischman, John. *Phineas Gage: A Gruesome but True Story About Brain Science*. Boston: Houghton Mifflin, 2002.

Hudson, Briony. *Medicine: A Magnificently Illustrated History*. London: Big Picture Press, 2022.

Ignotofsky, Rachel. *Women in Science: 50 Fearless Pioneers Who Changed the World*. Berkeley: Ten Speed Press, 2016.

Jenner, Greg. *You Are History: From the Alarm Clock to the Toilet, the Amazing History of the Things You Use Every Day*. London: Walker Books, 2022.

Kang, Lydia, and Nate Pedersen. *Patient Zero: A Curious History of the World's Worst Diseases*. New York: Workman Publishing Company, 2021.

Kang, Lydia, and Nate Pedersen. *Quackery: A Brief History of the Worst Ways to Cure Everything*. New York: Workman Publishing Company, 2017.

Kay, Adam. *Kay's Anatomy: A Complete (and Completely Disgusting) Guide to the Human Body*. London: Puffin, 2020.

Kay, Adam. *Kay's Marvellous Medicine: A Gross and Gruesome History of the Human Body*. London: Puffin, 2021.

Morris, Thomas. *The Mystery of Exploding Teeth and Other Curiosities from the History of Medicine*. London: Dutton, 2018.

Mould, Steve. *The Bacteria Book: Gross Germs, Vile Viruses, and Funky Fungi*. London: DK Children, 2018.

Paxton, Jennifer Z., and Katy Wiedemann. *Anatomicum*. London: Big Picture Press, 2019.

Payne, Kev. *Gross and Ghastly: Human Body: The Big Book of Disgusting Human Body Facts*. London: DK Children, 2021.

Tiner, John. *Exploring the History of Medicine: From the Ancient Physicians of Pharaoh to Genetic Engineering*. Green Forest, Arkansas: New Leaf Publishing, 1999.

Wakelin, Daniel. *Revolting Remedies from the Middle Ages*. Oxford: Bodleian Library, 2017.

Washington, Danni. *Bold Women in Science: 15 Women in History You Should Know*. New York: Rockridge Press, 2021.

INDEX